THE

OF TATTLETALE

BIRDS

THE CURSE

OF TATTLETALE

BIRDS

ROBERT J.

COVER DESIGN BY LEEANN OSSOLA
COMPILED BY LUCIE OSSOLA

XULON PRESS

Xulon Press
2301 Lucien Way #415
Maitland, FL 32751
407.339.4217
www.xulonpress.com

Unless otherwise indicated, Scripture quotations taken from the King
James Version (KJV) – *public domain.*

Printed in the United States of America

Paperback ISBN-13: 978-1-66282-986-4

Ebook ISBN-13: 978-1-66282-987-1

PREFACE:

Being laid up with a broken leg was driving me crazy with boredom. Then this extraordinary enlightenment thought came to me! An answer, out of the blue and I knew what I was going to do. I started to write this tale and it came together with great ease flowing from my memory and thoughts. Using many true events along with imagined incidents, that brings to life the journey of a young boy to his adulthood.

INTRODUCTION:

This tale begins as a child who learns that birds tattled on him to his very own parents. Then these tattletale birds continue to tattle on him about his actions. In his own mind creating this evil curse. Until this child acts against these tattletale birds, to save himself and protect all children from this evil curse, the battles are real and life changing!

TABLE OF CONTENTS

THE CURSE OF
TATTLETALE BIRDS

BLAMING THE BIRDS

CHAPTER 1

After turning and walking away from that large kitchen window with perhaps a grin on my lips, where I was watching my two youngest children outside in the yard. As I move away from that large kitchen window, with each step, came mixed emotions of pride, joy, and pain. What have I done to my youngest daughter by imposing this burden of such an evil curse upon her? And yet I could not help myself from allowing my thoughts to escape so freely from my mind, with each step, to this precise moment in time, back to the beginning of this evil curse of mine! Which it became years of battles with these witty creatures that spy on young innocent children, violating their privacy, their livelihood! The weight of this burden bearing down on a child with intense emotional aversion to own at such a young age and is heart wrenching. How can wise parents impose such an evil curse upon the innocent child they love, their precious treasure of life? What almost became the end of me, I now have passed this curse to my youngest daughter; can she survive what almost destroyed her dad? These memories from long ago still bring chills down my spine. Yes, so long ago; to time pass, way back in time, when I was a young child.

We all possess the capabilities of time travel, without the aid of a man-made machine; however, we are limited to traveling only in time pass. We can travel only in time

1

pass of what was and what is left to remember. The future is only a goal, dream, or perhaps a journey that has not been set in time. In our own mind, we can travel years past, to that precise moment we are seeking out, deep within our own memories, stored in our own thoughts, to multiples memories at the same time, and back to the present time, only losing a blink of an eye, a moment in time; yes, years back to a time of an innocent child about to make a choice that will alter his very livelihood.

I would have to say I did have a good childhood. There were many highs, along with lows, bumps, bruises, accomplishments, and spankings or whippings; yes, there is a difference between the two. Now in the front room, I reach for an old photo album in the closet on a shelf, where the photo album has been there collecting dust, out of site. I have not even given this photo album a thought in many years as I wipe off the cover and sit down on the couch. I open the old photo album, along with my youth memories of a time long ago passed. The furthest length of time my memory ushers me back to is an exceedingly small town just off a two-lane highway on the southeast side of this state.

As I began to look at photos envisaged the journey down memory lane; yes, this is a small town. It is longer in length, north to south, than it is in width, east to west. To the very west end, in the middle of town, is a single floor schoolhouse all by itself. Moving eastward one block, there is a line of homes a mile long next to a paved road, coming and going from the north and south end of town. Fifty feet east beyond the pave road, there is a railroad track dividing the town in two. Fifty feet to the east of the railroad track is another line of houses, half the length of town, next to a gravel road.

This gravel road would only be half the distance of that paved road. However, this gravel road went to that two-lane highway on the south side, right next to our house and business, then to that paved road at the north side of town.

There was a population of about 100 to 150 people that lived in this small town, which was larger in its coal mining days long ago. With the closing of the coal mines, some people had to move onto other places, to other coal mines.

We lived in a mom-and-pa store, large gravel parking lot, gas pumps, groceries, small bar, and restaurant with an attached home in the back. There is only one other store like ours in this town. This was such a great place for a little boy to start his life, where his innocent imagination could flow wild as the wind blows. Oh, we were not the richest family, nor were we the poorest family, by no means, although we did wear a lot of handy downs. It was just the way things were back then; it was a different time and a different place. You knew your neighbors and their families, as they knew you and your children; a closer community. Life was slower then much harder than it is today, and the world was just starting to spin faster.

There are new inventions that would change the family's way of living; better, faster, than ever before. People's ears must have been ringing with all the new promises of technology, of a better tomorrow. The application of scientific knowledge to distribute man quality needs has taken off and the world will be a better place to live. Heck, some houses had running water inside the home, while some still had toilets outside the house. Go help the neighbors shovel coal down their shuts. Rid yourself of that coal and that entire filthy work; buy a new gas furnace and you will not have to wash your walls again. Now that you have gas in your home, you can modernize that place with the top-of-the-line gas water heater, with hot water you do not have to boil on that coal and wood-burning stove. Look inside that large catalog and see that new gas range; four burners on top with a large oversized oven; oh, shoes are on sale.

Some of my favorite inventions, the telephone and the television; man, is this world starting to grow so fast; what an incredible time to be alive. Sixty years ago, we traveled by horse and buggy-covered wagons. If you had the money, there was nothing like the speed of steam-driven locomotive engines. Now, as a little boy, there are diesel locomotives, automobiles, trucks, airplanes, and jets; what is a jet? Man has flown among the stars. Man has walked on the moon! The adults of that time witnessed some incredible feats of man's accomplishments! What could the future possible hold, what inventions are yet to come, and what effects could they possibly do for mankind? Yes, there were naysayers back then: did man really walk on the moon, or was it a Hollywood fabrication? Hollywood; what's Hollywood? I would overhear and take part of some amazing conversations between people whom I have never seen or met before, at our store. Then, they were the ones that came in all the time and always had something to say, and some who wanted to be left alone to drink their coffee and eat their meal.

People were not as educated then; some would have to work at a young age, without the chance of a high school education. In these small communities, there were not many comforts that all people would have. I can remember the black-and-white TV, and Dad buying and installing the colored plastic sheet you put on the TV screen; the brown color on the lower part, then the green color above that, and on top, the blue color; the static electricity would keep it in place. Turning your black-and-white TV into a color TV. Yes, this was a complete failure, and Dad threw it away.

This town had no movie theater, only the two stores, and had no city park. Yet, in a quiet small town, time does move slower. It was different back then, most local people said little, and people were taught not to waste. If your big brother did not wear out those pants or shoes, and you fit in them, well, good; you would have another pair of pants or shoes. Our family was large as a lot of families were back then, and our parents...well, they did some cool things with us.

Our dad was from the old country. He was about five-feet-ten-inches tall, and 160 pounds; very muscular with silver hair; your average-looking dead, except for his age. He was fifty-seven years old when I was born, and twenty-seven years older than Mom. He had a simple rule of thumb: "If I catch you breaking the rules, you suffer the consequences!" We had running water, inside toilets, TV, and as a younger son, I did not have the responsibilities my older siblings had. I did not have to feed the chickens or dogs, work the restaurant, gas pumps, or the store. In these types of businesses, you had to have factotum workers, including your very own children.

Not me. I could play as much as I wanted to, and we lived in such a cool place to do so. To the west in the back of the house, past our yard, were the train tracks; to the north, was a field a half-acre in size, all the way to the church. Ah, the weeds there, at times, were so high I could build tunnels through them. To the south was another smaller field, which did not have many weeds. To the east was the extremely dangerous two-lane highway, and beyond that was a little creek. I had many great adventures while living there, and even the town we moved to a few years later brought journeys to amazing hidden places that only a child knows and loves. A child mine is a wonderful fantasy making brain that knows no boundaries.

My imagination, at times, well, I guess you can say I had my share of some unfortunate incidents. I flip more pages of this old photo album, now looking at old pictures of when I was young. There I am, about ten or eleven years old, with crutches under my arms. We were living in another town then. There is another photo with what looks like a cast on my right arm. If memory serves me right, I was a daring little boy who believed I could do anything and everything. Oh, the courage I possessed back then, or perhaps a little boy who did not understand or even think about the dangers. I had many a hospital trip, doctor visits, broken bones, stitches, and many other types of injuries and illnesses. Again, I flip another page in this old photo album. I am about three or four years old; a handsome little boy with a great smile on my face; happy, since I am on crutches again. Oh yeah, it is around this time of my life when it all started, which will become years of wit in battles against some of Mother Nature's wisest and devilish creatures. I can still remember my dad's words the first time he told me he could communicate with these spying freaks of Mother Nature. I was just a little boy and did not know what to make of this. I still had a hunch it was the older siblings that ratted me out. It happened again, and then again, and I know the older siblings could not tell on me all the time; they were not there. Weeks later, my mom admits she has the ability, to communicate with these winged deadly spying creatures. How could it be that my parents have this ability to understand these creatures, and I cannot?

I tried to be their friend, but I could not understand them, and why could they not understand what I was saying, or perhaps they choose not to listen to me? Why did God give these creatures speaking abilities that my parents could understand? Why do these creatures of Mother Nature pick on me? As I get older, oh the pain and hurt I felt when my teacher admits she has the ability, and they told her what I did.

The hurt went deep, within the very core of my being, and I could not speak. This changed everything. It is one thing to let parents know, but it is another thing to involve my teachers. What is so hard about all of this is, at times, these Mother Nature creatures prevaricate to the adults. Yes, my very own mother and father believe these creatures over their favorite beloved son! Teachers would believe these untruthful creatures over innocent little children. I know some of these spying creatures can see great distances; however, they have a brain as big as my thumb. I would have no doubt into the assurance of victory over these creatures of Mother Nature and put these freaks of nature in their proper place.

Growing up in a large family teaches the younger ones how to manage many types of situations, and how to survive the moment. Sometimes you need to cry and cry louder than the other sibling to be heard. Maybe all you had to do was point. At times, all you had to do was be quiet and shut up. Sooner or later, the attention would turn to the older sibling; where were you, what were you doing, were you not watching them? Yes, as a younger child that was so cool, and I love it, until the older sibling had left, and now, I was the older sibling; it was not so cool or fun then. The oldest would tell on us younger siblings when they caught us, or even point the blame my way when they did not know who did it.

It all started in that little town. I was around three or four years old. I had seven older sisters and one older brother; all were of average size. I had one younger brother and sister, but it was that one sister who was just over a year older than me; it seemed she would tattle on everyone but mostly on me, trying to get me into trouble all the time. With a large family comes multiple personalities; loud ones, quiet ones, daring, shy, tattling, mischievous and know-it-all ones. I came walking around the south side of the house and saw that one older sister was pulling my younger sister and brother into the house off an upside-down bucket. Through the open window, their journey went, with the passage looking like fun to me; however, when I got there, they closed the window and refused to open it and pull me through. The teasing started. They were not going to allow me this passage; they must still be mad at me, or at least that older female sister was.

Earlier that day, I was working on my tunnels in that large north field of weeds that was my fortress. This fort was protected with a Winchester rifle, like the rifleman used; a six-shooter the Duke himself would be proud

7

of; a plastic Buck knife a mountain man carries, Army helmet, and a stick horse named Trigger, tied up in the back. There are two escape routes going west, one toward Grandma's house, which was across the tracks on the left. The other on the right, looking at the tracks and to the north; enemies could come from there; the spying tunnels overlooking the church and the entire north, two more tunnels to the south one to the front of the store, and one leading to the backyard. There are many joining tunnels with meeting places throughout the weed field, a great place for adventure. The body will overtake the daydream as the thirst for adventure, changing the thirst to wanting a cold glass of water.

As I left the fort and approached our home, my two younger siblings, and that one older sister, are playing in a little mud pit. It appears to me that they were making mud pies. As I get closer, I asked if I could play. "No" was the response from the older sister. I did the little boy whine, asking again. "No" was the response. As the older sister picked up her fat juicy mud pie and acted like she was eating it, she asked the other two siblings how their mud pie tasted. The teasing had begun, and just like her, she knew which buttons to push.

An imminent power starts to energize within me and build strength when that older sister opens her mouth to take another pretend bite. POW. It hit. Half the mud pie enters her mouth, and the other half up her nose and onto her face. She jumps back and comes to her feet. Discarding that juicy mud pie, out of her mouth that she has just bitten into, she begins cleaning her nose and face. Oh, those frightful words every young child dreaded to hear screams out, sending chills down my back, "Mom! Dad!" I did what all little boys should do at that age. I turned and ran for my life. Serpentine, serpentine, she may be chasing me, fake left, break off to the right, faster and faster and break left toward my fort. I turn to see if she was behind me. No, she was just standing there watching me run, and then she turns, heading toward the house; she is going to tattle on me. I abort the escape run to the fort; they will know I will be hiding there. I head to Grandma's house. No, wait. She is not home today. I will turn left again to the chicken coop. I can hide behind there. We all know hiding is when a child uses the thought process and reasoning to come up with to explain the actions of one's self. I got it; a gust of wind came up and blew the mud pie into her mouth and face; no, that will not work. How 'bout she tripped over her own feet and fell on the mud pie? Are the younger ones going to rat on me? A bird flying by almost hits me in the head as I dunk, watching it fly away. I got it. A gust of wind came up and blew a bird into her hand, knocking the mud pie into her mouth. It could happen so fast the younger ones did not see the bird; yes, I could blame it on a bird. Then I reached out to knock down the bird but missed. Why did I run away after it happened? Because I tried to catch the bird, so they could see it.

Birds are fast and hard to catch; aw, yes, I am going to be ok. I was onto something now; everything was coming together. I was going to blame it on a bird. Birds are fast and hard to catch. Ah yes, I was going to be OK. I just needed to put on that little boy's face on for my mom; yes, this would work. That breeze, which was blowing this excuse into my thought process, also reminded me of my thirst. I still have not gotten that drink of water. Out from behind the chicken coop, I sneak like a skilled Indian brave to the south side of the store peek around the east corner of the building looking north to the front of the store. The coast is clear, but I better wait a while longer.

While in my thought process, I was deep in processing the birth of reasoning that I could not hear my parents calling my name to come home. I would be telling the truth that I did not hear them if they so asked me. Maybe it was better to go through the back door and into the kitchen for my drink of water. So, I peeked around the corner to the west looking north, and that is when I saw my siblings going through the window opening.

While standing outside that window, and then that one sister started to tease me that she would not open the window so I can pass through. So, now it is my turn. I cry out those frightful words, "Mom! dad," and I turn and run back toward the way I came from, turning the corner, when it hit me, and I stopped dead in my tracks. I bet they are coming out of the window again. I turn around and peek around the corner Sure enough, my older sister was lowering the youngest down from the window. I shout out, "Caught you!" and started to run toward them. Surely, I would make it into the window now.

I was a little boy still learning distance, plus speed and reaction time. I got there too late and the window shuts in my face again. I made it all the way to the top of the upside-down bucket. Here comes the teasing, the pushing of the buttons, and an imminent power starts to energize within me and build strength. POW. It hit the window, breaking it into pieces! Everyone in the room lets out a scream, then those frightful words shout out: "Mom! Dad!"

I did what all the little boys should do at that age; I turned and ran for my life. I ran toward the chicken coop; no serpentine. I head toward the fort. I am in the clear now as I hide deep inside the fort next to the pile of rock grenades. Then, I notice I am injured.

My right hand had small cuts on it and one deep long cut. Most kids would have started to scream when looking at it, but I have been here before. I was to afraid to make any noise. I did something bad, and I did not know what to do, did not know where to go. When I was looking at that cut, I could remember the first time I got stitches; flashing back deeper into time pass.

I was not supposed to go with the older siblings that day, but I tagged along like a big boy. They were headed across the highway to go swimming in that little creek; all of us, except for the two youngest siblings and that one older sister that liked to tell Mom and Dad what everyone was doing. I just started to earn my colors with the older ones. I was still younger than that one sister, but I was not a baby anymore.

I am a little boy who could start tagging along. This was my second time going with them, and I was happy as can be that they let me come along. We were not at the creek long as I was walking to get a bottle on the other side of the creek. I stepped on something, and it hurt; a snake or spider, perhaps; one bit me. I turned and jumped back, but there was nothing there. One of the siblings shouted out to me "You shouldn't be there. That's where you broke bottles last time." The water started to turn red as I was standing in it. "I found blood," I shout out. What kind of discovery did I stumble upon? Will I find a body, an animal...ouch, as my left foot was starting to hurt?

I picked up my left foot, and my siblings started to scream! I looked at my left foot; it was cut, and blood was pouring out of it. I started to cry while the others were screaming at me. I did not know what to do. One of my older sisters picked me up, put me on her back, and I hung on to her neck as we started to head home. "My shoes. Get my shoes." I will get into trouble if I leave my shoes by the creek. When we crossed the two-lane highway, I could see in their eyes we were all in trouble. Now, one of the oldest would surely be punished for this mishap adventure, and I may never get to go with them again anywhere.

I do not even want to go home now; everybody will be mad at me. I will not be able to hang around with the older siblings anymore—just as I was getting accepted into their circle to be a bigger boy. Oh, those frightful words shout out again, "Mom! Dad!" followed by my name, "He is hurt again!"

Our dad came outside as we neared the front door; oh, we could all see it in his eyes. He knew something went wrong and somebody was going to be held responsible. He saw me being carried, and turned back, going into the store. Dad was an old miner, and worked many years in the coal mines, and there were no injuries he had not dealt with. Heck, he could set or stitch his own injury and go back to work. Now, Dad came back outside with his miner first-aid kit, and perhaps there was a grin upon his lips. I now knew that I was in trouble, and I was no way near as tough as Dad.

Our dad could make you cry when giving you a haircut; his hands were bad from many years of work and play, from broken bones and dislocated fingers. So, Dad never really knew how hard he was pinching, squeezing, or holding your flesh and bones. He proceeded with this skilled first aid and questioning the siblings on what happened: "Who was in charge over there," and "This is how you should clean this wound."

Oh, the pain, oh the hurt; Dad looks at me, then tells me to "Stop being a crybaby; you're not going to die." Dad is squeezing my big toe so hard I think it's going to pop off! Dad sticks things inside the cut, cleaning it. I think it is tearing the open cut larger. I did not like his burning red cleaning agent; crybaby. It hurts. I am in severe pain. Here I am, a little boy, and it hurts. Our mom comes out of the store. "What has your son done now?" she asked our dad. Every time I did something wrong or I got hurt, I was my dad's son; when everything was good, and I did something right, I was my mom's son. Dad was rough and tough and the boss of the home; however, our mom knew how to take care of us when we were sick or feeling down. Our mom was a very caring, loving mother. She was shorter than Dad, with exceptionally beautiful long black hair, and a little overweight. Crybaby? I have been called a crybaby before by many people, and a doctor, who thought I should be as rough and tough as Dad. While Dad and Mom worked on my cut foot, I flashback deeper into my thoughts to the first time I was called a crybaby by a doctor, and there could have been a grin upon his lips.

The doctor looked similar, to my dad appearance; a short stocky man with little to no hair and wore small glasses on his face. I was having stomach pains, and Mom told Dad, "Your son needs to go to the hospital." "Oh, he is fine; just a virus." Dad replied. After what seemed like days and the pain getting worst, Mom insisted, "You are taking us to the hospital now." Mom did not know how to drive automobiles, and never did learn in her lifetime. In those days, there was only one way to check for appendix, and for a little boy, it was nothing but pain and shock. No, I do not know how big that doctor's fingers were; the pain, however, was gigantic. Oh, the pain, oh, the hurt. Doctor, please get your finger out of there!

Yet this doctor stated, "You don't need to be that big of a crybaby." I don't care. I want my mama; she will take care of me. Oh, by the way, thanks, Dad, for bringing us to the hospital that day; my appendix did break, and if we had waited much longer, things could have been much worst.

They had to do emergency surgery, and when I woke up, my mom was waiting there; although, not for long, as she had to go home and feed the other siblings. Later, a nun comes into my room. I know who these people are; they work for God, and are genuinely nice people, but what is she doing here? The nun is an older, tall, slim woman with robotic movements. Just then, another lady walks in my room; much younger than the nun, probably a teenager short and thin with bright blue eyes. She was wearing an outfit with pink stripes going up and down on a white background, even on her hat.

This is starting to look good for me. I think this other lady is going to give me ice cream or, perhaps, cotton candy. I have seen these outfits before. I believe, at the fair or maybe at the carnival, with all that I have been through this day, and now I am going to get some ice cream. Perhaps cotton candy; please have strawberry ice cream or blue cotton candy; maybe I can get both. Oh, the pain, oh, the hurt. I did not get anything but pulled out of bed, and it hurt; you must walk after surgery.

Walking up and down those long cold hallways is painful; then, just as I got used to walking, we went back to my room. Now I must sit down in a chair. No, just let me stand here; but now I am sitting in this chair; that was so much pain for little boy to go through. When the nun and her pink striped sidekick returned, they wanted me back in the bed; now for the life of me, why do you choose to hurt me? "I want my momma!" I cried out. It is one thing to be called crybaby by your siblings, parents, or even a doctor, but it is different when the nun calls you a crybaby, along with her back-up psychic teenager in pink striped uniform. My mom gets back, and I am in safe hands now. She knows how to take care of me.

Oh, the pain! My foot is on fire with Dad's red liquid that he is brushing onto my wound. Dad is done with his first aid and training class to whoever wanted a lesson on that large cut on my left foot, which included not only siblings but also a couple of customers. With my left foot all bandaged up, they are now ready to take me to the hospital for stitches.

I do not know if it is better to wait out for the possibility of getting punished or to get punished right away. Is it worse to wait or is it better to get it over with right away? Dad and Mom are taking me to the emergency room, which is about five miles away. The older siblings will have to wait to find out who will be held responsible for this accident as they watch the store till Grandma gets there. Oh, sorry older siblings, for that mishap.

This doctor with a large finger—I do not know if he ever numbs any of my wounds before stitching them; it always hurt. Oh, the pain, oh the hurt! The doctor also likes that red stuff, and is he trying to make me as tough as Dad? Now I may be wrong, but there could have been a grin upon his lips as he stitched away on the bottom of my left foot while talking with Dad. This will not be the last time he would stitch a foot of mine, nor would it be the last time I would see blood in the water.

As my thoughts wonder forward in this time past, we were lucky to have television in our house, especially at the time of the Olympics. These men were jumping over a tall bar attached on two poles; they were using a pole that bent a lot, but did not break, to fly over the top bar. Then, these other guys were jumping on a board, doing flips and landing in a swimming pool. Wow! I am off to find a pole I could be jumping over fences, maybe onto the roof, even though I am not allowed on a ladder or the roof anymore. A branch will probably work better than a pole; it could bend. It just needs to be large enough; then, I trip over a board in the backyard near the woodpile. Hey, this board will work to jump in our swimming pool like those guys did on TV. It had some black oil or maybe tar on it. I did not know what that black stuff was, but it should make it a better board. I drag this board over to the pool a few blocks, here and there, and it is ready to try out. I quickly go into the house and change into my swim attire; I want to be the first to do this.

Our pool was just one of those plastic ones that came out that year; it is about ten inches deep or so, and about seven to nine feet wide. Well, I will just run to the end of the board, jump as high as I can, back onto the board, then spring into the air; this is what they did on TV, and this is what I decide to do. While in the air, I will then flip forward or backward. I put my arms up, just like they did on TV, took a deep breath, ran to the end of the board, jumped up into the air, and back on the board. Oh, the pain, oh, the hurt! And I ended up doing a frontal flip, landing on my back in the pool.

As I sat up in the pool, my right foot is in severe pain, and something is protruding out of the water as the pool water is starting to turn red with blood. I raised my right foot out of the water, the protruding object following, along with a scream that started to come out of my mouth at this shocking sight I am witnessing. Apparently, parts of the diving board I thought were so thoughtfully assembled, entered deep into the bottom of my right foot, breaking free from the board like a prisoner from their cell, and attaching itself to the bottom of my unwilling right foot. This would explain the lack of height from such a leap of faith in hopes of winning gold.

As a little boy, having a small foot with what used to be fine quality lumber, about twelve-inches long and one-inch wide, sticking out of the bottom of my right foot, is truly quite a shocking sight! I knew I wanted my momma; I had to get to that back door and into the kitchen as fast as I could go. I am still a little boy learning distance, plus speed, and reaction time. Oh, the pain, oh, that hurt! I did not clear the side of the pool because of the additional length of attached lumber to my right foot; although, I may have removed some of the extra loose pieces of wood from my foot. I did not care to look back at the pool. I got up off the ground and hopped toward the back door. The look on my mom's face and some of the other siblings was devastating. *Am I about to die?* I thought to myself.

With some of my siblings starting to cry and the tears in my mom's eyes, I knew it was over for me. With so much to live for—if only God would give me one more chance. I would have done so much more for Him. I guess my screams of horror earlier had set the ball in motion. Yes, Dad is on his way with his trusted miner first-aid box; if only he gets here in time. One of the siblings is telling Mom that Dad is waiting on the customer, and when he finishes with that, he will come. Oh, can I hang on long enough? I do not want to die. I am so afraid this is the end that I am squeezing my mama so tightly she is having trouble breathing. I could hear the other siblings shouting, "Hurry up. Hurry up, Dad!" and then there he is; there could have been a little grin upon his lips as he looks at this injury. "It is ok. You don't need to be a big crybaby; you are not going to die," Dad tells me as he starts to examine my foot. Dad wants all the siblings there for this first-aid training lesson; however, this time, he must send a couple of the older siblings out to run the store, since customers are here. Oh, the pain, oh, the hurt, as Dad used that red stuff on my injure foot.

We are waiting for Grandma and Grandpa to come across the tracks and watch the store before we head to the hospital. Mom's hands were still shaking as she was getting things ready. On the ride to the hospital, I am praying that doctor with the large fingers is not there. Mom and Dad were not having the best of conversations. Mom is gabbing about holy dirt in some church in another state, a blessing, a guardian angel to watch over me. Dad states, "We really need more eyes on this kid. For Pete's sake, this kid was on the roof, throwing rocks at customers and their cars last year. This kid has to be watched, like a hawk watching for its prey; bird eyes—whatever it takes." I know it is late, but sorry, Dad. I should have not thrown those rock grenades off the roof at customers and their vehicles.

Although, it was I who saved us from the invading army with those well-placed grenade rock tosses from off the roof onto tanks and army men; unwillingly, it was also then that I learned the difference between a spanking and whipping. And why I was forever discouraged from using a ladder or being on the roof again for the rest of my life. Just my luck; that large-finger doctor is here at the hospital again as I am placed onto a bed.

The medical staff starts to study this unusual site of what was a fine piece of quality lumber at one time, now protruding from the bottom of my right foot. As word passed throughout the emergency room about this peculiar incident, I had many a visit to my room. Several hospital staff came in to witness such a site; some making strange faces, and then long discussions on what type of actions were needed. Even a couple of maintenance men came in and shook their heads. And now, this doctor with the large finger comes in, looks at it, gives instructions, and I think I there is a grin on his lips. I wake up, and I am in this hospital room with another kid, and those pieces of protruding lumber are removed from my right foot.

It has been too long I cannot remember why this other child is in the hospital, but it is nice to have company. The next day, they take him out of the room, and that large-finger doctor enters the room, carrying a jug with red liquid. Three nuns and a different pink striped outfit girl follow the doctor. Doctor states, "I am going to paint your foot red, and clean it." The three nuns and that pink striped outfit girl hold down my arms and legs. When this doctor starts his torture of applying this cleaning agent on my right foot, there could have been a grin upon his lips. In church, and even the restaurant, you could hear stores of humans in dismayed situations, with an explosive inherent of Superman strength; freeing one's self from binding chains or large pillars. The nuns with their sidekick could not hold me down, and the doctor gave up.

The next time, the doctor came back into my room, and he was accompanied by four large men dressed in white, to do what the nuns failed to do: hold me down. These men were too strong and held me down while the doctor removed splinters from the bottom of my foot. This repetition of painting my foot red every couple of days continued until all quality of this fine lumber splinters were removed. That black stuff on that fine lumber that I thought would make the diving board better reacted differently in my body, sending spider web-like red lines up my leg, coming from where it once held that protruding quality lumber. Children do not pay attention to time, and I cannot state how many weeks I was held prisoner in that hospital. I wanted to come home to my mom. With the bird's land near me, releasing me from my memory journey of fine lumber hospital stay...back to my right hand that is cut.

Birds are flying in and out of the weed fort, reminding me of my plan. Then it hits me; this is the way out of this mess. I am still going to blame the birds. It will work; I have witnessed these stupid birds fly into windows before. My hand, how do I explain...yes, that the glass fell from the window, hitting my hand before I left to catch the bird. I must admit, some of my skills of reasoning came from watching the older siblings try to explain their way out of trouble. I think now I will not get a spanking or whipping, and there is a difference between the two.

Spankings are the results of a minor mishap after the parent high-court ruling, with the maximum of two swings, which impacted the stationary behind, depending on the results of witness and property damage, were mostly done with a bare hand or using a cap.

Whippings are the results of a serious mishap after the parent high-court ruling, with a minimum of two swings, which impacted the stationary behind, depending on the results of witness and property damage; moreover the swings can be increased depending on how many court visits one has had in that month.

Whipping verdict dictates a choice of tools, which could be a quality piece of lumber cut to aeronautics design, or the top-of-the-line American leather belt without beads. However, property damage dictates no less than two swings. All swings can be repetitive if one misplaces an arm or hands to block this swing.

Assured of success with this artificial fabrication of a great story of various events of a stupid bird that did not see the window, it could be fable in their eyes; my older siblings, who, in turn, will put me back in their circle when they hear this tale. Heck, they may come to me for advice when they get in trouble. I can go home proud and with confidence as I start to exit the fort.

The closer I get to the door, the more my confidence dissipates; with the increase of pain on my hand, *blame the bird, blame the bird*, I think to myself as I go through the now-closed store toward our door. That was always so hard to go home after a flee-in-flight ordeal, but boys will be boys; deep breath, stupid bird, as I open the door to the front room.

In my mind, many scenarios played out of the events that were about to occur; have I told you there is a difference between a spanking and whipping? I stepped into the front room, not feeling too good about my assured success. Simultaneously, all the siblings in that room stood up, without saying a word, and walked out of the room as though they were trained zombies, around the corner and down the hall; some, without looking at me, headed to the kitchen. The faint sound of whispering is now coming from the kitchen. I can hear Mom say, "You need to talk to your son." His son...oh no, *blame the birds, blame the birds*, races through my thoughts as I sit on the couch to watch TV. Then there was the sound of a chair pushing back away from the kitchen table, the first step being placed on the floor, sending vibrations that shake the floor in the front room as if a giant was on his way.

The purity of fear emerges from deep within, grazing on every cell while covering the body with invisible armor, restricting my very movement and speech. I am scared. Have I mentioned there is a difference between a spanking and a whipping? There is Dad. He paused for a moment, then sat down next to me. Dad sits in silence for a while; the bearing weight I am holding in is making me ill. I feel like a man in this picture, hanging in the store, where he is holding the whole world on his back. "Let me see your hand," Asks Dad in a tantalizing relaxed voice. This was the first time my dad spoke to me when one awaited the results of the parent high-court ruling. The results were always read first in a stern voice, then the amount or type of sentence, then the action of sentencing incorporated to one's behind. This was then followed up with an infusing conversation about identifying the incorrect process of doing things and the direction for the immediate future; now go meditate on this action.

I picked up my left hand that was covering my right hand, slowly moving my left hand toward Dad; not sure if he was trying to trick me with his relaxed voice. "Other hand" with a sterner voice from Dad as Mom walked into the room. As his crushing grip of a strong man that he is, starts probing my wounded right hand before the pain, before the hurt can start, in an instant, I remove my hand from Dad's grip. Deep within you is your spiritual heart and soul, sacred vault of your being, ascension the guiding force of your life. God place wonderful unique characteristics there and gave us the ability of thought processing. An imminent power starts to energize within me and build strength. POW!

I jump off the couch, look up at my dad, right into his eyes, and started to speak this tall tale of these devilish birds. The words came out of the blue and starting to flow out of my mouth with ease like a mighty river coming down from a mountainside. "This devil of a bird breaks our own property, and shall be held accountable for such devious actions, and brought to you, if only I could have captured it!" I shout out. For I have now stood in front of the parenting high-court ruling, speaking, for the first time, without the judge silencing me before the completion of my statement. This court is in shock for this little boy wallows in victory, standing before the court with pride and honor; stories of this day will be told for centuries to come. Children will be speaking of this day of a child's victorious speech in the parent high-court ruling. I have become a legend, as popular as a king; children will know my name for the rest of time.

Oh, the pain, oh the hurt, as my dad grabbed my arm, leading me to another chair, and sets me in it. You can hear running down the hallway as the siblings were listening to what was happening. Sticks and stones may break my bones, but names will never hurt me. This was the first lecture from Dad, and Mom I received a long time ago, without a spanking or whipping. And words will hurt just as much, if not more, than the physical parts when they are spoken from people you love and respect. You know the pain settles deep within you, in that sacred vault of your being, where your heart and soul lays. You contain certain desirable qualities, which are gifts and traits place in you by the Heavenly Father. These are the things that make you unique. As you grow in maturity, learning the differences in what is right and what is wrong, then doing what is in your heart. Those are some of the statements from the lecture I received so many years ago, in doing what is right for the family, and I sat there and listened. "Do not ever come into this house, look me in the eyes, and lie to us. I know what happened today, and your siblings did not tell me anything."

"The birds you are trying to blame, flew over to the front of the store, landing by the pumps, and told me everything you did, from the mud pie to breaking a window. The birds, tattletale on you and they will do so again. I told the birds that they could watch you and tell me if you are up to trouble. You will start to feed and water them every day, along with the chickens and dogs. Idle hands are the dev-il's workshop". Those are some of the words stated in that lecture. I would always try to do what is right, but things did not go as well as they should; perhaps for the lack of planning. When the inner pain dissipates, at bedtime, I did have trouble trying to sleep that night.

Many times, after a child get into trouble, you have extremely hard nights, with little to no sleep. Sometimes the fear of death would make you wish you were never born at all. Where is Jesus? Why can't Jesus just come to save us all now! That bedtime prayer I did not like: "if I die before I wake, I pray my soul for you to take." I will not say that prayer, but I pray for forgiveness of all my wrongs, including lies that I told. I prayed to keep us safe and healthy. There are many fears in a child's bedroom, from monsters to animals. I slept many times with a blanket over my head. Then there were the other types of sleepiness nights of excitement and joy.

Those words my dad spoke of earlier kept me tossing and turning; the birds told him! My dad can talk to birds! The excitement of this leads to so many thoughts of joy: we are going to be rich my dad will be on TV; I wonder if dad can teach me to speak to the birds. They can lead me to the gold and diamonds in the mountains; we are going to be rich! All the things we could buy...With all these wonderful images rushing into my brain, I did not sleep much at all.

Well after a few days into learning that bird language proved to be impossible for me; the frustration starts to overcome me. These stupid birds knew nothing but whistles, chirps, peeps, squash, and shrieks. I gave extra food and water, made many noises back to them, and used a whistle of mine; nothing worked.

I am starting to think the birds do not like me because I blamed them for breaking the window and pushing that mud pie into my older sister's mouth. Watching them eat all the seeds I threw out and listening to them, it is starting to sound like they are teasing me, pushing the right buttons. An imminent power starts energizing within me and builds strength. POW! The sound of breaking glass echoes through the air.

I did what all little boys should do at that age, I turned and ran for my life, serpentine head toward the back door. I was still grounded from the fort, so I could not run there. As a little boy, I was still learning distance, speed, and reaction time; the rock I picked up, disregarding, toward the unwisely birds, had quite a bit of lift to it; overshooting its intended target and impacting old windows on the chicken coop. Oh, the pain, oh the hurt! I have mentioned that there is a difference between a spanking and whipping.

There were three possibilities how Dad became knowledgeable of the broken window events that occurred that day. The birds, my younger brother, or that one older sister tattled on me. First, my younger brother will be the target of revenge; he must learn that you do not tattletale on brothers, no matter how many swings of punishment you get of two swings or less. If the verdict of the punishment was more than two swings for a brother, then it will be ok to save oneself and let the story be told. The planning was far more superior for the ease of this task at hand; almost a waste of time.

Simple plan: get the nickel empty bottles from the storage, line them up by the chicken coop, get grenade rocks by the railroad tracks, and get your younger brother. These are the bottles you get a nickel for turning them in for a refund, and there were lots of empties. The plan is enforced upon younger brother, who has a better arm than I, to challenge him to see who can break more bottles. As the breaking begins, I tell him I am going to get more nickel empty bottles, as I seek out an innocent victim to witness such a terrible crime before our eyes from the actions of our younger brother breaking these bottles. Unfortunately, there are none to be found as I head back to where the rock-throwing contest is going on.

Dad comes around the corner with my younger brother's ear in his finger, grasping hard enough that my younger brother's face displayed that of much pain. Sorry about that, younger brother. All the superior planning could have not been this good; luck played its hand on this day, while looking for an innocent victim to lead over to where this terrible crime of our younger brother was committing this crime of breaking bottles. To have this witness see with his very own eyes and not be a sibling; it would become Dad! I think to myself, *I got to be the most intelligent child that ever lived in the small town; soon, my parents will be asking me for advice.* Later, Dad calls me over in a tone that might possibly want me in the parenting high court ruling to help with judgment of such crimes. I run to him with the fastest speed my legs will carry me. I am honored to receive this privilege that has been bestowed upon me. Oh, the pain, oh the hurt! You know there is a difference between spanking and whipping. Again, these creatures tattled on me, and I am starting to hate these devilish tattletale birds!

I would like to think I was my mom's favorite child; my younger brother was the baby of the family and got treated like so, but still, my mom loves me more. When birthdays came around, we would have special cakes with the birthday person finding money in their slice of cake; in those days, fifty cents was a lot of money, and a great thrill to search out your piece for the hidden treasure. I always got extra from my mom, a larger slice of pumpkin pie, cake, ice cream, and more at any meal. I would always get something more.

We did make this trip to that church in another state. If my memory serves me correctly, this church had this blessed soil, giving blessing to people who would go there, and remove soil from this incredibly special blessed hole.

It was a long trip, but when we got there, I was excited to see this hole that never gets any deeper, no matter how much blessed soil is removed from it. Inside this church there were lots of crutches, casts, canes, and clothing hanging from the walls. A line of people from the outside leads into this church, which, in the center, has this hole of blessed soil. People were filling cans and cups with this blessed soil from this hole and taking their blessed soil with them as they left the church. As we reached this hole and it was our turn, Mom made me get into this hole as she and whoever else standing nearby dump cups and cans of blessed soil upon me, covering me from head to toe.

I was the only child of the family that got this extra helping of blessed soil on this day. Other people looking at me with wondering faces, *why is this action needed on this well manner child?* As we are making this journey to the center of this church, no other people had the thought of bathing their children in this blessed soil, a dry baptism.

In hopes of saving a child while there; collecting blessed soil to fill cups and cans. In fact, on this day, I witnessed no other child forced into this hole of blessed soil. Our family filled up cups and cans of blessed soil for each one of us, and we left. Although, on the way back home, Dad took a turn a little wide, bouncing from one side of the two-lane highway to the other side, then back again to the correct lane of travel. Everybody bouncing around inside the van and all got a little bit of blessed dirt on them, and, perhaps, with a blessing, keeping the van from flipping over.

We always traveled in a large panel van in those days, with block windows on the sides; it eliminated any arguments for who gets to sit by the windows. If I recall correctly, there was a mattress in the back for the children to lay on if they got tired. I would love listening to the drive through the speaker for the large orders the family would order; that always got the person to say through the speaker intercom, "Can you repeat your order, please?" On our trips, I was the child mostly watched by everyone, making sure no mishaps would happen, from knocking over mannequins, or slapping people of whom I did not know. On our trips, as we got into the van, we would do a head count, making sure all children were present before heading out to the next stop. On one trip, as we left a gas station to return home, we did the head count, kind of late on the family members, like we always did; however, this time, coming up one short; having to find a spot on the road to turn around and go back to retrieve the quiet younger sister left behind at that gas station. She received much-needed hugs that day, but Mom would always give me extra hugs, candy, and smiles; therefore, it hurt me even more when I found out Mom could speak the bird language, understanding these evil birds.

I happened across some change in the kitchen: two pennies, two nickels, and one dime on the table, along with four freshly baked pumpkin pies. I love pumpkin pie, so I proceeded to taste each pie, searching for the best pie among the four. I have not taken anything over to Grandma's house in a long time; she would like one of these pies. It was a tough call to make; they are all tasted delicious. However, I did pick one pie after numerous samples from each pie.

Mom will be so proud of her son; of his thoughtfulness and caring deed he is about to perform. I also take the remaining change to place on the railroad tracks, turning small change into larger change. In the backyard, heading to Grandma's house, birds are in my way. I stopped to pick up some ammo, almost losing the pie. These dreaded birds are getting on my nerves. I set the pie down, and then throw into their flock a handful of rocks. Mom is now calling me from the back porch; maybe she wants to add a bowl or ribbon around the pie. I picked it up and marched back, with knees lifted high up by my chest, back straight, like an army man would do, and a proud smile as big as the blue sky on my face.

Oh, the pain, oh the hurt! There is a difference between a spanking and whipping. That one sister sibling was with Mom in the kitchen when I got there, but I know it is not her tattling on me. I am lost, confused, beaten, sick to my stomach, and I am in shock as Mom states the facts, that she can speak to these tattletale birds, and is getting upset with my actions.

The parent high-court ruling banned me from speaking on this day, as the facts are being quoted by the court that these so-called creatures of Mother Nature witnessed this crime against me. An imminent power starts to energize within me, build strength, and POW! I stand up and shout to the parent high-court ruling: "Mom, I am your son!" The parent high-court ruling has no mercy today, and I am pulled away from my mom; the cord has been cut, and her favorite beloved son has no say.

Has all this misery started with blaming of these tattle-tale birds? These creatures are not of-God creations, but toys and puppets of the devil's choice, trying to destroy our love. I am mad as holy, and will not take this any-more, for this curse the devil has placed upon me will be defeated, and I will break this curse.

There will be no other child that will have these freaks of nature harassing them. I have underestimated what these tattletale birds are capable of and will not make this mistake again. Mom and Dad believe these freaks over their beloved son, as my heart falls to its lowest point ever. Have I lost my mom and dad's love? Will I lose my siblings' love? Where has this divine evil power of these creatures come from, and why have they brought this curse upon me?

Depression is real and can affect a young child. How will I be able to fix everything to where it was before? I am a prisoner in my own house, and only allowed freedom to the outdoor world when I feed these freaks of nature, the chickens, and dogs. These birds do not appreciate the bird seed, nor the water placed outside for them. All the taunting noises they make toward me, pushing the buttons—an imminent power starts to energize within me and builds strength. POW! I cannot take it anymore! I declare war on all tattletale birds. I will break this evil curse placed upon me. I hate all TATTLETALE BIRDS!!!

By Robert J.

WAR OF THE BIRDS

CHAPTER 2

As I flip another page in this old photo album, there is a photo of our home next to that two-lane highway. This photo triggers my journey back to the facility in my mind where memories are stored, to that exact moment of time past, when this photo was taken. Yes, so long ago, when there was talk among many adults about a new super four-lane highway coming through our town, right in front of our home. As a child, I imagined that there would be super cars on this superhighway. I remember Dad shutting down the store for the day, and, sometimes, we would sit outside on benches in front of our store while counting vehicles on the highway driving by. You would learn to know the different makes of the cars and trucks, and their colors, along with keeping count of the differences. This could be so much more fun on that superhighway, and the super cars driving on it. When construction started hundreds of miles away, the plan went in a different direction, moving the highway further away to the east from this little town.

These new plans would not include an off-ramp to this town, which was devastating news to this community. Mom and Dad had much conversation about this, even the talk about Dad selling the business, retiring, and moving to another city. All this news means to me, I do not have much time, as these tattletale birds are my adversaries;

this war now must be quick, deadly, and humane; survivors placed in aviary as my prisoners. Showing the devil, along with these freak-of-nature birds, there is no curse, and this type of behavior is not acceptable!

My siblings' behavior toward me then was not much better as the teasing started, making fun of me because of the action of these creatures of Mother Nature. "What is this," "He did what," "Thank you so much for letting us know," came their aggravating taunts. "The birds told on you, the birds told on you, and you cannot go to your fort anymore; you cannot leave the house." This is a tune that started to get to me. At this rate, it may be years before I am allowed out of the house and out to the yard. The fort will need plenty of work, as I long for the freedom, along with the ventures the fort brought me.

Then opportunity knocks; my sisters leave their room in a hurry, leaving their top-of-the-line plastic dolls out. The dolls with legs, arms, and a head that could move to different positions, lying on their bed; totally ignoring the rule that when done playing with them, put them away. An imminent power starts to energize deep within me, building strength. POW! I remember the teasing, pushing of buttons, the tattle telling. I start to quickly remove the arms, legs, and heads, from the dolls, and throwing some pieces out of the window, some all over the room, then taking the rest with me to be discarded in the backyard. I do this with amazing skill and speed as the last piece falls from the air into the chicken coop, as though I am feeding them.

Loud screams start coming from the home, those frightful words every little child dread to hear: "Mom! Dad!" I did what every little boy that age should do, I turned and ran for my life, serpentine to the right; no, I am not allowed at the fort. I turn and head south and around the house to the front of the store, passing birds that I could have thrown something at. I continue running north to a bench outside in front of the store to sit down on, and I made it in time with no one seeing me.

We have these benches and chairs out in front of the store, where I am sitting and catching my breath, when I noticed lots of birds and lots of good ammo, but the front of the store is off limits, remembering the invading army war. I am not even sure if I could be outside, but I cannot sneak into the house from the back door. There is still screaming and crying going on toward the back of the house, which reminds me of what I have done. I have been on this bench before; hearing screams coming from that two-lane highway and ditch.

In fact, sitting on this this very bench, counting cars, I have, more than once, heard that devil screams of a lost soul, along with her children shrills during the night, scaring all of us; what seemed like only weeks back.

You see, in these parts of this country, we have a living dead legend: the dreaded La Llorona! The legend is, this tall skinny woman in a white gown with long black hair, searches in the night air around rivers for children and adults to take and bring them to water, drowning them with her own hands, then handing their soul to the devil.

Some say La Llorona was born to a poor family in a small poverty-stricken village of which it did not even have a school, and no longer exists because of the evil games that were possibly played there. She was said to have spent her days in her poor home and in their dirt yard in the front of the home, but one day, a rich man riding by caught site of her beauty while she was outside.

The two quickly married without much of a court-ship, and within a few years, had two children. The rich man travels for his business, but on his returns home, he began to pay more attention to their children than to his wife, which resulted with their marriage coming to an end. The rich man came to visit his children when he could, bringing them lots of gifts. One day, he came to visit them with his new wife, and they wanted to take the children to spend time with them at their home. This did not go over well, and La Llorona, with her children, left the village, never to be seen alive again.

Three days later, a villager went to retrieve water, and found her two little bundled-up children, drowned in the river. Some say they drowned through her neglect, but others say that they have drowned by her own hand because of her jealous hatred toward them. There are different stories of this evil soul-seeking woman. She lost her mind, went crazy, playing around with the devil's ways. Not wanting her own children, for the freedom she seeks, bundling them up and throwing them into a river, drowning them, losing them forever. Then changing her mind, chasing after them, only to lose them to the river current and to drown herself. Making a deal with the devil, she now hunts for children's souls to repay the loss of her children's souls to whom she promised to the devil. The soul of these two children went to the Lord's home, for they had done nothing wrong. Allow your mind to expand and heed this warning: as the sun gives way to the night, stay clear of rivers and ditches, for La Llorona is searching for souls to take.

Her children's souls had been saved, so do not fall for bundled-up crying babies or young children's screams near rivers to save and bring home. For La Llorona uses these cries of children to lure people to these non-treasure's traps. However, she gets a better deal if she takes the favorite beloved child soul away from the family! It was here, while sitting on this very bench, when out of the dark night air, came the wails of screams from a small child; La Llorona's baby! These screams are high in pitch, with lower squeals lasting until all air was expelled from their lungs, only to inhale the much-needed oxygen to start over again, hoping that someone would come! When life is over, the screaming will cease. Do not go searching for death; you may find it, and whatever you do, do not bring it home! So, on that night of counting cars, what did

Dad do? Dad gets his trusted flashlight with his sidearm and seeks out this devil trap near the highway, down by the creek, to rescue or silence these piercing cries of life expiring.

We were bouncing around as though the earth's soil was nothing but hot charcoals under our feet, while the screams of emotional and physical pain continued to echo throughout the night cold air! Mom gathers her flock, escorting us through the store and then into the front room. I pray that Dad gets back unharmed and without this devil's trap, for the soul the devil seeks to seize is mine. I am the favorite beloved child. This was the first time I heard wails of screams and cries piercing one soul of life ending. But as time passes, I will hear La Llorona's children's screams of terror a few more times, and always by the highway near the creek.

Each time these screams would happen, Dad would challenge this devil's trick with his trusted flashlight and sidearm, in search to stop these horrific screams! It is one thing to hear La Llorona's baby's screaming wails through the night's air; it is another thing to hear La Llorona herself!

One peaceful evening of counting cars was interrupted with the screams from the depths of hell itself; this was La Llorona piercing screams! La Llorona is cursed, seeking souls for all eternity, never paying her dues, for they are too far to grasp, and far too many to accomplish. She will trick fools who follow in her footsteps, playing with the devil's ways, collecting their soon-to-be lost souls, and the unknowing brave, who are lured to her needed screams and cries for help! Let the truth be known, for I have heard La Llorona, with evil-piercing screams and cries that were extremely loud, clear as the night sky; causing the back of your head's hair to tingle, like pins and needles prickling into your skull! That ended up sending shivers down my spine as though ice itself is melting there.

Crying high-pitch screams of horror, then a shout in a pleading voice, "Help me! Please, someone help me!" echo down the arroyo, across the creek and highway, coming from the ditch near the old coal mine, where the new highway will pass through soon.

The night air turns cold, so now you can see your breath; the soil below your feet heats up as the burning charcoals are now present. Beware, for evil has arrived; evil is here! As we are bouncing around Mom, she gathers her flock again. As the shrill-piercing screams of emotional and physical pain of life that maybe ending soon still echo out for us to absorb, for us to hear, Mom escorts us through the store and into the front room. The action was quick that night; Dad on the phone, then got his flashlight, along with his sidearm, and soon a sheriff's car showed up. Then Dad went with the sheriff deputy out into the cold night air filled with darkness, up by the old coal mine. I pray for my dad to come home safely, and to stop gambling with the devil, for he is needed here with us. I would never know what happened that night, but there were many whispers between Mom and Dad about what took place, and even a thank-you note was left upon our front door. Therefore, I would never play beyond the sunset near the arroyos; there is no need to take a such a daring chance.

"Hey," my older brother is calling me. "Dad needs your help," bringing me out of my nightmare of La Llorona's daydream. I spring into action, for it is not often he requests my services; in fact, this may be the first time, or, perhaps, maybe we are just going fishing.

Oh, the pain, oh the hurt! There is a difference of a spanking and a whipping. I hate tattletale birds, even though I was in the wrong to dissemble my sisters' dolls. Oh, by the way, sorry sisters, for that were wrong of me to do so. Being reminded again that these birds are not going down without a fight, I must now use my complete brain capabilities to plan the end of these devil tattletale creatures.

The wit sometimes need pressure to be creative, or perhaps I am giving these birds too much, though; after all, I have been feeding them. That is the answer I am looking for: poison. I can poison the feed, even the water; will God understand my actions? God may not like this, for other creatures could fall from the poison. This war is on tattletale birds only; do all types of bird's tattle tale?

Remembering Dad's words that day in the car: "bird eyes"; was Dad talking about all birds, small to large ones? This becomes overwhelming to me; so many birds to engage. Do just some bird's tattletale, or all of them? It just must be the birds that hang around the houses that are the tattletale birds. What kind of poison should I use since I cannot read? I just know the things under the sink are poison, but which one is best for these birds? I decide to do what I do best; ammo—I need lots of ammo.

The best ammo is in the front of the building; however, because of the invading army war, a place I cannot play, remembering the parent high-court ruling, the railroad tracks will have to supply this war. I can bring all the rocks I need in a small bucket, then dump out near the fort area. Buckets, for now, were plentiful.

I still have that hidden change that I found on the kitchen table from the pie ordeal. I better retrieve them, since I am going to the railroad tracks. For those who have not placed coins on a railroad track, they are missing a transforming site.

These coins will be doubled in size but not in value, unfortunately. In fact, they will lose all value once owned. It is still worth the value of the coins to witness this crushing sight, as I carefully place my coins on the track where I should be able to find them later after the passing of a train.

This is a place where we have done it before with great success of retrieval. When an idea gives birth in one's brain, it may lead to greater places than one has not thought about. So now, I start to place larger rocks on the tracks; the train will cut them down into smaller rocks to supply my ammo. Wait, if I place branches on the tracks, they could be cut down into arrows and possibly spears when a train passes by; now the tracks are getting loaded up with branches and rocks, when an imminent power starts to energize deep within me and build strength. POW! It hits me!

We are going to be rich! Mom and Dad will be so happy; we will have all the money we want. I should have thought of this years ago as I head toward the pile of wood in the backyard. Birds flush off the ground by the wood pile as I think I have found a hiding spot of theirs.

On top of the wood pile is my diving board; I was wondering what happened to it. All this wood is going to work great. I start to carry and drag boards as fast as I can to the tracks; carefully placing them in specific angles and degrees in my building of a spectacular derailment trap of a train wreck toward our home. People will come from all over the places to see the pileup train cars in our backyard and, perhaps, we will be able to sell the photos of this wreckage of train cars!

The train tracks blockage is starting to become a massive sight as l turn for more supplies.

We could even sell tickets to view this train wreck, when I see two men at the corner of our fence. Wow, people are starting to show up already, to watch, as I wonder how much they will pay me to watch this train wreck happen; wait, that is Grandpa and Dad. I should have done what little boys do at that age, turn and run for my life. I thought they were going to be happy. "We are going to be rich," as I explained this well-thought-out plan, then executing this plan from rags to riches idea. This is the first time I had to clean up a project before the parent high-court ruling. Grandpa made a statement loud enough so I could clearly hear him speaking to Dad, "If it was not for those birds flying over and telling me, we could have a big mess here." These birds know this is my grandpa. These tattletale birds can talk to Grandpa. All these devil tattletale creature...why do they pick on me? It was fun walking home with my dad and grandpa holding my hands, and at least till we got home.

Oh, the pain, oh the hurt! There is a difference between a spanking and whipping; this time, it even hurt in my heart. I have greatly underestimated these tattletale birds; they can speak to any family member of their choosing. To win this war, things will need to change. I will need help.

Yes, the adults in this family can talk to the tattletale birds and believe them, how can I get my adult family members to believe me over these tattletale birds? Sometimes, help comes from places that you would least expect it to. It was almost a blessing; I am back in the war with confidence of winning, thanks to the help of my older brother's friend.

At that age, I have no understanding of time. I knew when it was time to eat and to go home before the sunset, but, mostly, I knew it was time when I was told. I knew seconds turned to minutes, minutes turned to hours, hours turned to days, days turned to weeks, weeks turned to months, and months turned to years. I knew when my punishment was over; they would tell me, and sometimes it felt like years.

My memory of this time is like missing pieces to a puzzle; you can still see the finished product, but how you got there is missing a few pieces. I can remember a baseball, roof, and a gutter on a building near the church. Either way, I have a small cast on my right leg below my knee to the end of my foot, where my toes are sticking out.

The exact reason is lost forever in my brain, missing from my deep thoughts, misplaced in my memory, although I am, again, on crutches. I finished setting up a trap, which was a box held in the air on one side with a stick under it, which, of course, has some string tied to it.

I saw this trap on TV to try to catch a rabbit or bird. Now I am just waiting on tattletale birds to get to the bird seed I placed there under the box, pull the string, and bingo, I can catch one or possible more birds. This war has not given any favorable outcomes to my side so far; maybe this may change that score.

My older brother's friend is waiting outside for my brother when he checks out my plan to catch a bird. Then he showed me his matchstick shooter made from a clothespin that my older brother and he had been making. Yes, this was a fine piece of weaponry, as he demonstrates the use of these fiery missiles of flames launched into the air by this shooter. This craftsmanship was that of a reversal use of the spring technology of the clothespin; cock the spring back to where it stops in place, then insert a wooden match into position, and fire away; wow, amazing! He has a few of them with him and lets me have one with the condition I not to tell anyone where I got this shooter; this is a done deal!

This is wonderful product, simply made, and now, all I need is burning missiles ammunition, which there is a box of wooden matches in the kitchen to light the stove. After grabbing a handful of wooded matches, I get out of the kitchen without anyone noticing I was there.

I am ready to fire missiles out to practice targets placed in hidden areas of the yard. I will need much practice for an assault on these tattletale birds. There are some weaknesses with this magic weaponry. The distance is that only of a few feet; sometimes the missile burns rapidly and goes out before impact. This means an up-and-close personal assault with these devil creatures, and feathers will burn quickly. Of course, I did take a few practice shots at the chickens; sorry about that, chickens. Now, I know the plan must be simple: go to the tattletale birds' hiding places in the backyard near the railroad tracks by the pile of wood; there, I can possibly see the tattletale birds on the ground, for a sneak attack, since my mobility is limited on

WAR OF THE BIRDS

these crutches. I pass the get-rich site on the train tracks, nearing the ambush location, where the birds are possibly hiding on the ground, which is near the southwest corner of my fort.

There they are; not hiding, but feeding, not knowing I am near and ready to fire upon them. Still learning distance, speed, and reaction time, I first shot a little low and to the right, as the tattletale birds take flight. Oh no! A fire starts at the missile crashing point; quickly, I put the shooter in my front pocket, and am up on crutches, a couple of hops and kicks of dirt, and with the heel of my cast, I push dirt and begin stomping, putting the fire out. A few yards away, another sneak attack and another shot; oh, just high, the birds take flight and another ground area ignites. The distant, speed, and reaction time, along with the use of my leg cast to extinguish this fire just builds confidence in me, as I wonder if the fire department boots are black-painted cast; another shot, another miss, another ground ignition. I put the shooter quickly in my front pocket, come up on crutches; a couple of hops, a push of dirt, and a stomp with the cast extinguishes the fire, with much increased reaction time. Yes, the challenge is on, baby; these tattletale birds are in trouble now!

There are some large, taller weeds inward on the fork boundaries where some birds are sitting near the tops of these weeds; their backs are toward me. Quietly, I maneuver to a shooting position, like an army man; I peek up and there is a clear view all the way; the bird is still unaware of my coming surprise attack. I removed the shooter, kissed a match, and loaded it in place. This bird will pay for all birds with the big mouths that like to tattletale on me! There is a slight breeze moving this large weed, as a bird rock gently back and forth. I rise, get the flow of the motion down, aim, pull the trigger, and the missile is launched; with great ignition, a good flame, the line of sight is on the target; oh, so close! The bird turns in time, duck the flaming missile, while taking flight off this large weed.

There is an old saying: "Kids who play with matches get their fingers burned!" That burning missile crashes into the bottom of that large weed, igniting the weed; with the shooter in my front pocket, I jump on crutches with a couple of hops, and in a flash, it just went out of control.

Now, I wonder if Moses's burning bush was as large as this bush! Abort the fireman mission; the weed in front of me is infernal. Flames higher than my head and every-thing around are catching on fire; all the other weeds are starting to burn. I did what kids at that age should do; I turned and hopped away for my life, no time for ser-pentine, and I move as fast as crutches would take me. I enter the backyard, past the back door, and I turned to look. I would have fallen to the ground if it were not for the crutches under my arms.

"No, no!" I shout out. "Not the fort!" I did not know if anyone was over there. Mom comes out the back door with a laundry basket, dropping it; then, she looks at this now great fire. Weeds burn hot and rapidly all the way to the ground; in a moment, all is lost. There is nothing left of the fort! They are using a hose behind the church, put-ting out what is left burning. Dad now has a shovel and someone else with him using a fire extinguisher, which they are all working on to extinguish this fire.

Other people start to show up as they go through the burning areas, putting out smaller fires, and then, here it comes: an imminent power starts to energize deep within me, build strength, and POW! It hit with such a force; everything I had eaten or drank in the last week came up, repeatedly, until there was nothing left, but I continued to gag, getting every drop out, leaving the taste of failure in my mouth.

These evil Mother-Nature-creature tattletale birds have tricked me into burning down my very own fort; they led me to the fort, like a puppy dog on a leash. I have lost everything, and they are out there; they are all laughing at me. Are these tattletale birds indomitable? I have been suckered into the devil games! I have been played a fool!

Why has God led me down this road, into this battle of witty tattletale birds, and I did not get any help from Him? I am a beaten boy. I have no more will to battle these tattletale birds. I am starved to at least come close to winning one battle. Just let me get close to winning one battle! I am losing every battle; now, losing everything I have built in that fort. An imminent power starts to energize deep within me and build strength, POW! Hate has taken over me for these tattletale birds. No, I will not give up. I have lost many battles already, but I have not lost the war; too many children are depending on me to win; maybe even God Himself.

I have moved away from my regurgitated mess to the fence; however, the pain is still in my stomach. I have lost everything. The rifle, pistol, knife, Army helmet, and the stick horse named Trigger; the fire destroyed all of this! People are coming by to look at the burnt field. I do not care if I could sell anything that may be left right now. I am still in shock. The volunteer fire department is at the scene, and one fireman is with my dad as they slowly walked by, pausing for a moment. I overhear them talking.

"The people at the church were painting the shed, when a big flock of birds came up, making all kinds of noises flying, having the workers look this way, and saw the fire. Lucky thing they were painting that shed in the back; they quickly got the hoses and started to water down everything, stopping the fire there. If this fire jumped over to those trees right there and moved down the ditch, half of this town could have burned down. Thank God for that flock of birds flying up and making all that noise." Kick me while I am down; these birds started this fire. They are not the heroes. They are the devil's tools of destruction.

Am I the only one in the world that sees these creatures for what they really are? When you lose in such ways that I have, hate is being born within you, and as evil is giving birth, it is hard to control, and I am a little boy with so many of these thoughts arriving in my brain. So, when Dad comes back toward the backyard after thanking the fireman, still carrying his shovel, still moving dirt to throw on hot stops, then Dad comes over to talk to me. Dad looks down at my feet and asked me a few times, "What happened to your cast?" removing me from my deep evil thoughts building inside my brain. "What?" I replied. "Your cast. How did it get all black and dirty? I did not see you in this field." "Empty your pockets" came his next request. Wow, the life is being sucked right out of me now as I look down at my darkened black cast.

You know there is a time in one's life that you will feel many emotions at one precise moment in that time, such as shame, foolish, embarrassed, and or stupid, or all of these at once. I do not want to empty my pockets; why is all of this happening to me? What have I done? Why are all things out to hurt me? I tried to hide the shooter and the matches; however, they are spotted within my hand and pockets. As I am being escorted to the home by an ear pull, the questions start to come out: how did I become owner of such weaponry?

Oh, the pain! Oh, the hurt! There is a difference between a spanking and whipping, along with no pity from the parent high court; crutches or casts makes no difference today. Oh, sorry older brothers' friend about the information slipping out of my mouth that I could not keep close. I am sure a parent was called about how this weaponry found its way to me. Beaten, done, no more, and nothing left in me; too much to handle for this little boy. I am, again, a prisoner in my own home, and now my parents are questioning my mental wellbeing; what is wrong with this kid? Is he broken? Is he mentally sound?

The only comfort I get is this black and white TV. I can watch but not touch to turn the channel. When you are young, TV can make many impressions on you; is this real or fake? Do you or can you tell the difference on what is being shown? TV is my only benefit while imprisoned; at least I was not grounded from watching it; just the great outdoors were off limits again. After leaving my bedroom where I was doing puzzles, I came into the front room, and it finally happens to me there on TV.

A big colorful bird was talking, and I understood it! I stopped and watched the TV; shocked that it was talking to its owner. "Hello," it would say to anyone that entered the room. It had a name and would ask for a cracker. "I want a cracker." I cannot believe it is hungry and telling you what it wanted to eat. It even wants kisses from its owner. I now know it is possible to catch and train these birds so everyone can communicate with them.

I must get to the outside to talk to these tattletale birds. But before I can get out of the front room, "Don't be a fool," the bird states. I stop and look at the TV, then it starts to whistle and chirp; again, it states, "Don't be a fool." I head toward the back door, wondering what that meant. I was born with a hearing loss, and had trouble, at times, articulating words. I cannot get any bird to talk to me, and did that bird on TV just now call me a fool? The hearing loss was in my left ear; did I hear that bird correctly?

I remember having to travel with Mom and Dad to another city about 100 miles away, which was much larger than our little town. We would go to a building, where this woman would help me learn to speak better. Across the road, there was a zoo, and, sometimes, you could see some of the animals that were outside in their fenced-off areas. I am not sure how many times I went to this building to learn to speak better, but I do remember the last time, and how it ended. I could not hear the sound this person was making; therefore, I could not repeat it, no matter which position I placed my tongue. This woman would not listen to me, and just kept pushing me to make these sounds that I could not hear! An imminent power started to energize deep within me and built strength. POW! It hit me, and I bit this person's hand. She would not stop making these sounds with her tongue, and shaking her hands, to listen to me explain why I could not do this. I could hear all the words that came out of her mouth very clearly after I bit her! Sorry to this person who was trying to teach me to speak better. I should not have bitten you. As we left the building, birds were outside, chirping like they were laughing at me for what I just did.

I am again getting close to having my freedom again, so I must be careful not to get caught; days go by, but no response to my efforts of communicating with these tattletale birds from open windows or even peeking out the back door as time continues to pass. Although, at times, I would sneak out when my parents got busy with customers and try to talk to these birds, but they chose to ignore me, acting like dumb birds. When one is doing his or her time in punishment, in quarantine, you lose all awareness of time, until you hear that you are free, and the outside awaits you; your excitement of freedom has come!

It is genuinely nice to see the exterior of the home again, but extremely hard to look at the burnt fort field. I continue to collect rocks, piling them up in hidden areas around the backyard, and, when possible, throwing rocks at tattletale birds. Knowing I will need help to outsmart these tattletale birds, I try to involve my younger brother into this war, but he will not join in with me. I pray to God for help, for I cannot win this war without God. I need help in every way possible.

My birthday is always a great time; we had the coolest money cakes ever! Then turkey at Thanksgiving; I love pumpkin pie, and Mom always gave extra to me. The Fourth of July was great; Dad would sometimes light the city fireworks display, and we would get a front-row view of it and what it took to send these explosives up into the sky, along with a ground display of fireworks of many wonders. Ah, Christmas, every child's favorite time of the year, and we would have so many gifts because of all the children; we would run out of room under the Christmas tree.Out of the blue, at times, one would receive gifts with no meaningful day; could these be blessings from God not understanding the reasons why?

These gifts can come by friends, family members, or strangers, as was this unexpected gift that I just received. My older brother shouts out to me, "Here, you can have this, just do not tell anyone," as he tosses a homemade slingshot for me to catch. It is made from high quality heavy gauge wire, bent into a U-shape, with the handle tape for a better grip; with rubber bands attached to a loop made on the frame of each side of the slingshot, then attached the other end of rubber bands to a fine piece of a leather pouch. With this fine tool, the strategy of the war now changes to my advantage. Where you are now is a starting point to where God is taking you; is this why God has me collecting rocks for ammunition and piling them up until needed? All these devil tattletale birds are in trouble.

I was so excited to receive this gift. I did not think of why, at first. Is my brother giving this fine piece of weaponry to me to set me up? Perhaps he lost his mind and did not know what he was doing. A divine gift should be accepted and not questioned as I just forget about all other thoughts. I must be careful with this tool, knowing what could happen to the shooter, and what I will be shooting at.

Practice makes perfect as my skill starts to develop into a sharpshooter. I got to a point where there was nothing to hit—can on the ground or fence at a reasonable distance of a few feet. My first trial and error was the ammunition; flat rocks are easy to pinch in the pouch. The flight is uncontrollably breaking off the straight path in all directions. The round heavy rocks do not have great travel distance; the little rocks moved with great speed, only to slow down and drop off from the air. The best ammunition was from the gravel on the side and the front of the store; its flights had the birds nervous. The collection rocks from this area will need to be cunning and quick for me. I am forbidden there, at the front of the store, for a long time because of the last invading army war.

As my skill grows in closing the distance, along with my aim, it will not be long that I will take down a tattletale bird. My aim has improved to where I can take shots at flushing up tattletale birds; it is so close I can taste victory. The birds are also learning about me as they start to stay farther away and flush up before I get close enough and do not feed in the same area, even leaving the bird seed alone that I placed out for them. My preparations of advancing with the skill of shooting has left me behind the birds; they will not stay close anymore. However, I did come up to a solution for this problem: I needed more power for my slingshot!

At our house, there was almost everything that you could possibly need. A handful of rubber bands were in my pocket as I ran outside to install more rubber bands on each side of this sling shot. I have tripled the power and doubled the range. I believe this war will come to an end soon. Now, will these birds open communications between us, in making a truce, freeing themselves from the devil ways?

All children will learn my name and the battles I have fought. I may become as famous as the last sling shot fighter in the Bible; the child, David, who used a leather sling and a rock to bring down and kill the great giant warrior, Goliath!

We could get rich; people can call me to shoot lions and bears where they live, freeing them of fear. Although I am a fair warrior, I will try one last time to speak to these evil birds before the rock bullets start to fly.

Outside, I approach these tattletale birds on a fence and shout out to them; "Stop tattle telling on me and all little children, and I will not bring injury or death to you; we will live together in a truce that I will honor." There is a lot of chatter going on, but I cannot tell what it is. I ask again, "Do you understand me, and if you do, speak to me so I can understand you."

These birds are not going to talk to me; in fact, the only bird, that colorful bird on TV was the only bird ever to talk to me, and the last thing it stated to me was, "Don't be a fool." I have done God's will to try to end this peacefully, but tattletale birds are ruthless, and they chose war.

Little do they know of my new weapon improvements in my back pocket. This war is back on again; let the fighting began. To the victor belong the spoils, and the loser will fall. I have not tasted the sweetness of victory in these battles, and I long for this taste. I will not fail again, having tripled the range and speed of these rocks that about to give new birth to this war.

This speed is shocking the birds; they start chirping to each other in warnings that death is on its way. This stronger slingshot adds smite to the rocks and should end this war quickly. These projectiles are coming extremely near to the tattletale birds barely missing them, and the birds are in panic mode. When you least suspect it, things change. A brave tattletale bird shows up, landing on the south side of the store, daring me to shoot at it, keeping a distance between us so that the shot can go either way. Nearing a possible impact with a flying projectile, the bird ducks and shakes his head, then just hops a few more feet away from me. I am closing the distance again, walking backward; the bird jumps the shot and flies up as I turned to shoot once more, just missing so close that feathers may have fallen off this bird. This bird flies in a circle and lands again, in one of those blind spots toward the front of the southeast corner of the store. I could load my pockets with more ammo since I am getting low. I am moving in a serpentine angle, confusing this tattletale bird, nearing it all along. The bird jump shots and lands again, resulting in another close miss, landing closer to that two-lane highway.

I am not allowed that close to the highway, so I move to the south and wait for a couple of cars to pass my line of sight and take this shot. Not bad. The distance is great with this slingshot with the extra power these rubber bands are supplying.

I take another shot at this same tattletale bird as it jumps up into flight, breaking left and landing again toward the front of the store, daring me to try again. This bird is still in range. I can take a shot, so I moved slowly toward this tattletale bird. It is starting to walk around the ground, heading toward the north to the front of the store, but I move as well, closing the distance with each step. This is it for this tattletale bird; now I am well into my range as I keep my back to this daring tattletale bird. I pulled back on my slingshot, and as I turn, this bird jumps to flight straight up, breaking left in a sharp dive and celebrating its speed. I had the tattletale bird in my sight with great follow-through and released the shot. To this day, I am amazed at the ability these birds have while in flight.

Feathers fly as this tattletale does spectacular acrobat contortion feats, as if no gravity will contain this bird movements when in flight; a dramatic event I just witnessed at dodging a speeding flying projectile to stay alive! This shot missed, so close to impact this tattletale bird; one could not fit a piece of paper between projectile rock and the bird itself. As I watch this miracle of display of movements as this tattletale bird continues to fly away, not to turn back this time, and land near me.

I did not hear that large picture window glass breaking in front of our store; apparently, many other people did. Looking toward the front of the store, there is Dad standing next to a car with the hood raised; he must be checking something on the motor. There is Mom with a customer, standing outside the restaurant door; wow, here comes Grandma.

Mom must be waiting tables as she has her apron on; then I see this large picture window broken glass all over the place; everyone is looking at me. I am a good distance from that window, so the power of this slingshot is incredible.

Then it all comes together like paper origami. I did what all little boys should do at that age, I turned and ran for my life. I throw all evidence from my pockets, dropping my magnum slingshot as well. I can run a lot faster without the cast, for it was removed a few days back, but I am still not fast enough. A single tattletale bird tricked me again making me a fool, leading me like a puppy dog on a leash, and, still, I was warned by a bird not to be a fool!

Oh, the pain! Oh, the hurt! There is a difference between a spanking and whipping. This time, I do not feel as bad; this was so close. This tattletale bird gambled with its life, narrowly escaping with its great flying skill. Oh, this bird may be a hero among other birds. Moreover, this bird knows this victory was only paper thin of a miss. Oh, yeah, sorry older brother, about that information that slipped out of me like an old man slips on ice; the pain is real. However, the lesson learned was you must look beyond the shot to keep the damage from happening.

With age comes the responsibility of reasoning on making proper correct choices, limiting punishment time of restricted freedom; yes, I have been a better boy while in prison inside the home.

I have not been called a crybaby in a long time, have not broken anything, been nice to my siblings, and my manners have been great, along with my listening ears of improvements. My daringness has been tamed. Winter has arrived, as I get to see the daylight outside again.

With my freedom while outside, I notice there is not as many birds hanging around like there was; word must have gotten out about my shooting skill. There has been much talk about moving as this superhighway nears our small town; to me, I do not care if it ever gets here. I am simply happy that I can be outside again, earning the trust from Mom and Dad. I have even been picking up trash outside without being told to do this. Mom and Dad must have noticed the change in me, and must be proud of me, allowing more and more freedom. Even the winds of faith come blowing my way, changing my misfortunes, in permitting more freedom than I ever had. I have long to go with Dad on his big-game hunting journeys, but I have been too young to go with him.

I have gotten to go with Dad and older brother on small game hunts and doing just fine in the listening department of life. I am not pushing any one's buttons, although I cried once; it was so cold, and I wanted to return to the heat the truck promised.

When I was younger, I would make a fuss, "crybaby fuss," for not being allowed to travel with Dad on big game hunts, or with Dad and older brother on small game hunts. I am starting to learn that big boys do not cry; just accept the fact and move on. Mom and Dad have noticed the change in me; after all, maybe I am not broken, I can make good choices, or maybe the winter blues have just slowed me down on rushing my thoughts. An older cousin comes over, wanting to go small-game hunting, taking my older brother and me along with him.

I am shocked that dad allowing me to go on this adventure, telling me "Go get your boots, jacket and gloves; you better listen to him." You would think I would have great memories of this hunt with great tales of success. I remember it was cold, very cold, way too cold, cold to the bone cold, and freezing cold. The best memory of that day is the return home. It was dark as we neared our home, pulling into that gravel parking area, coming up close to the door of our store. The headlights reveal that there is a vicious large German shepherd chained up, growling and barking at us while showing off his teeth. Wow, we got a new large dog.

Our dad was a character himself in his life, doing some amazing things, and you never really knew what to expect from him. I think I inherited some of his daring thoughts when I was born. We would come home at times to see many different things; in those days, if a truck would have an accent on the pass, people could go get the damaged goods, including injured animals.

Nothing went to waste that was still edible from canned goods, and even clothing; of course, it was the damaged goods that you can take. So, how did we end up with an adult German shepherd dog tied up to the store near the front door? Apparently, police dog trainers from a large city in another state were transporting trained police dogs to a larger city in this state to a police department. One of their canine companions was just not a good traveling partner, and after having to discharge from both ends of its body, creating a fragrance of poop and vomit combined, it then created a lot of gagging from the operators driving the van, which made traveling a bit difficult.

Only Dad could make this deal, saving this young-adult, trained police dog from possibly being abandoned along the roadside of a dangerous two-Lane highway because of its carsickness disorder. Needless to say, our family had another dog to feed, but this one may eat me.

It is tough to feed an animal that thinks you are his dinner, but I managed to get it done each day without getting bitten. With each day, the dog starts to accept the fact that I bring food and water to him. One must wonder if this dog is broke; is this beast mentally sound? Will he ever be tamed enough for me to take around? I think this dog and I are starting to have a meaningful bound with each other. We must keep this German shepherd away from the other dogs for a long time because he is mean and wants to fight the other dogs.

However, Dad wants to keep him because of papers of a full-blooded German shepherd. I do not know about that; why would someone want a mean young dog? I start to see this dog and I share a common hatred for birds, chasing them when they try to take some of his food. As time continues to move, I watch this dog many times going after these birds with only a blink of an eye from swallowing a complete bird in one gulp. With many more birds coming back from their winter hiding place, this dog is starting to get annoyed with them, still showing his angry side. As time passes, this dog has grown into a giant, and is more at ease with the family; mellowing out, and no longer has the need to eat one of us. I have seen our dad get bitten a few times by our dogs while trying to pull porcupine quills out of some of our dogs' faces.

Dad would have the dogs face between his legs, and with pliers, pull out the quills, and the dogs hated it, biting his hands while he was doing this. The dog clinic charged way too much money to remove quills from animals. Sometimes, more than once, Dad would remove quills from the same dog, for it did not learn its lesson to leave porcupines alone. When the dogs got ill with no cure, Dad would put them down, and as a boy, I had to witness this duty of ending a life of an animal that is part of the family. It was just the way of life back then; the men of the family would have to do this hard event, then bury this part of the family. These are some of the saddest memories I would have, which would include the passing of Grandpa and Grandma.

This giant of a German shepherd needed a name, but I cannot recall the name the family picked for him; however, I do remember the name I gave him: Tad. Tad is short for what his real name was: Trained Attack Dog; secret mission Tad. With spring in the air and birds coming back, plans start to come into my mind. I wonder if Mom will ever let me have my slingshot back, if I could train this dog like they trained bird dogs. Maybe the birds will not tattletale on me anymore if Tad, the giant of a German shepherd, eats just one tattletale. This plan can work, even if the tattletale birds tell on me. I have no control of Tad's menu of what he chooses to eat; only what I can feed him. As I watch Tad chase these tattletale birds, I start to cogitate; should I even try again after all this is a curse on me?

I have only come close a few times to ending this war on tattletale birds; maybe a time for a truce, then a sign is sent to me from above; it hits me like a rock; a big, long, wet, white and brown bodily waste discharge from a tattletale bird intentionally landing on my leg, barely missing my face; feces! The imminent power starts to energize deep within me and build strength. POW! I stand up and shout out; this war is to the death! These tattletale birds have no morals, no respect; the gloves are off, and all is fair in war.

This is a big pile of feces, and it is a gooey mess; hard to get off my pants as it soaks through, touching my skin, and what is up with all this bird chatter? Are these tattletale birds laughing at me? Do they know what buttons to push? I have now decided to do a secret mission: release Tad on unsuspecting birds. I wish Dad had let us know what the words were to get Tad back to a police dog for a surprise attack. There were secret words that one could not use around this German shepherd, bringing him back to his training ways. My training will be simple: rule number one, do not get Tad mad at me; I do not want to get bit. Rule two, have lots of treats for him; he is getting bigger around the waist area.

Rule three, use a long chain to start with. Using this long chain, I can take Tad around the backyard for walks, then, finally, down to a short leash. Mom and Dad are surprised to see me take this much interest in this dog, taming him down for walks. I believe Tad knows what this mission is about because of his own hate for these birds. I feel this mission is a go and start to put bird feed out by the blind spots on the south side of the building. Dad owns this south-side field that has no weeds on it. On the north side of the building, the burnt field that used to house my fort, is owned by someone else. I am no longer allowed to play or be on that property, so training must stay on the south side for the surprise attack by Tad. The winds of faith now have brought us together here; the battle will begin.

Bird seed has been in place for a few days, and we let the birds feed in peace. These birds have watched us go down there when they were feeding, then Tad and I running at them flushed them up. I keep Tad on this short leash when we run toward the birds, slowing him down to my speed. I place us just south of the feeding area; little do they know, this time, secret-mission Tad will go into effect. This time, I will unhook the leash and send him alone. Tad is ready, and what surely will become Tad's great victory. Mother Nature against Mother Nature, these tattletales have no idea of what is about to happen to them. Position is good, distance is good; look into Tad's eyes while unhooking him, then turning Tad's head so he can see the birds feeding. All that torment these tattletale birds have burdened me with, all this pain and hurt—it is now my time for victory. All the training, missions, failures; now come the time for this great moment; mano a mano; let the battle began. Children will be talking about this war for years to come; they will know Tad's name along with his great bird-fighter companion.

I wait for some feeding tattletale birds to look at us. I want them to see this coming when it happens. This one tattletale bird and I lock eyes into a deep hypnotic stare; this could be that same bird that led me to break the front window; it is a showdown look. I raise my arm out and lower it slowly down, pointing toward that one tattletale bird staring me down, and I shout, "Attack!" In the blink of an eye, it worked; the attack is on! The speed of Tad is that of a rocket propelled as birds are in shock as they attempt to fly, with that one bird who was staring me down being the last to react. The jaws of Tad snapping down as he tried to snatch that one bird as they break off hard to the east with that one staring bird lagging. Tad slips a little on the turn, his rebound is that of a great athlete; with each bound, he is nearing his target again; this is going to be close in catching a tattletale bird in flight.

That horrific awful sound every person dread to hear, and even worse, to witness where these sounds are coming from while taking for granted of what is. The screeching noise of applied brakes, tires sliding on payment, then the coming boom sound, followed by the two thumps, sound forever etched to one's memory for life. Oh, the pain, oh the hurt! I have just sent Tad to his death chasing that tattletale bird across this two-lane highway! This site of what had just happened cripples me as I fall to my knees, screaming, "What have I done?" These devil tattletale birds have no mercy on any life, and, again, lead me to destroying Tad! I could not move while Dad and this person driving that car went to this site of death, removing Tad from the highway. I do not know if the bird made it across the highway, nor did it matter; these tattletales played me a fool again. I pick myself up and slowly head to the backyard, wondering when we will bury Tad, or where. I stood in the backyard for a long time, tears running down my face, and with a broken heart.

These tattletale birds have no respect for property or property damage, nor do they have respect for any life! It finally happens in this war; life was lost, taken away because of me not looking past the shot. I did not have a command to stop Tad from running. I did not even think of it. Tattletale birds led Tad to his death as I watched; it was my fault for the lack of planning; out-smarting me again! Tattletale birds may have a small brain, but they have a large mind, and the help of the devil, becoming too much for me to handle. Why has God let me do battle without helping me like the devil helps these birds? Then an imminent power starts ener-gizing deep within me and builds strength. Pow! It hits. I shout out to these devilish creatures of Mother Nature tattletale birds, "Listen to me. I will avenge Tad's death. I will one day stand above a dead tattletale bird that I took its life!"

"Let it be known, I will snap this curse like a twig, and I will not falter, nor will I fail in defeating all tattletale birds. Let it be known to the world that I hate all tattletale birds!"

Robert J.

THE MOVE

CHAPTER 3

With a heavy heart of that horrific memory of losing Tad, I flipped a couple of more pages in this old photo album, and there is a photo of us loading up the truck for the move. Looking at this photo released the journey of time past being recalled to that very moment of time, and how the family felt in leaving behind our home. Human emotions are like pebbles in the sand on beaches, with too many to count in various sizes, shapes, and colors. In life, emotions, at any given time, can and will change with each breath one takes in various situations of stress, sorrow, and happiness. So, you can imagine the emotions of the family when the news came about the buyer of the business; Mom and Dad deciding to sell, along with a purchase of a new home in another town, just north a few miles away.

There is the emotion of excitement, anticipation, fear of new or the loss of old friends, and the loneliness of leaving behind a home with memories of what was. Yes, there were many emotions because of the move; maybe you are just too emotional; why do you show your emotions like that? Emotions can even be expressed in body language. Trying to hide behind a fake smile, the look of being exhausted, the trudge of shoulders, and the deep inhale of long breaths; the gleam in your eyes that shine from a big smile, the happy song one thinks of, to mention a few. For me, now five years old, I needed this move; most of my memories of emotions were of death, defeat, despair, and failure. I needed a new beginning after all that has happened to me; a new fresh start may do me some good; who knows, tattletale birds may not live over at the new home.

This new town is much larger but still considered a small community by standards of the state. This city sits in the foothills, and to the west, a mountain range forty miles from town to the north, east, and south are prairies, flatlands as far as one can see. The population is just under 8000 residents, much larger than the town we lived in before. There is a lot of construction going on with the building of a new school, hospital, and the new four-lane highway. The schools had more than two classrooms per buildings; one school, from what I hear, has a swimming pool in it. There is even a school behind our new house. I cannot tell you how many schools there were in this town, but there is one junior college.

This town had three movie theaters and one drive-in theater, along with three traffic lights downtown on Main Street, although, one of the movie theaters is starting to shut down. One of the last two open movie theaters had only Spanish-speaking movies, that I would go watch with Mom and Dad. One time in this theater, I won a large black-and-white stuffed dog when they called my movie entrance ticket number. I named this prize-stuffed dog, Tad. This town is more exciting than I am used to; however, I kind of end up with the same results.

We have completed the move and start to settle in the new place. Some of the older siblings have moved on starting, their new lives. This home is not as large as our other home, so the boys will have to share a bedroom, as did the sisters. We had a small front yard with grass, a small concrete side yard with a little backyard. This new house came with a large building, an old store in the front to the street, coming to an end near our front door. Dad puts lots of his stuff in there for storage. This building has a working walk-in freezer and some nice see-in-meat coolers; it also had a full basement, and in the back of this building, small living quarters.

This building is larger than our new home. Dad will only use this building for storage; never to open another store. There is a large city park with a small playground, only one block away from our new home. I have just started to meet new kids when an old acquaintance returns.

In these olden days, there are many homemade cures for many sicknesses: vinegar, garlic, castor oil, mustard, and potatoes, to name a few. Ah yes, the mustard pack on the chest, potatoes on the forehead; he is so hot he can cook these potatoes, which then leads to my old acquaintance, the large-finger doctor; he may possibly have a grin upon his lips in seeing me again. When one temperature refuses to go down with modern medicine, one is then forced in other ways of doctoring. They placed me in a tub of cold water, then with an added twist of modern-day technology, add ice, joining me in this tub. Let me tell you, this is colder than that rabbit hunt; not as long, thank God, but much colder. One starts to uncontrollably shiver, only to the point of freezing before you are removed from the ice bath.

I guess, it was only rightfully so that I had a few setbacks and spent more time in this old hospital before it would get taken down. The acquaintance of that large-finger doctor with injuries or sickness returned to spend time with me, sending me back to this old hospital. I would have a few more stays there. At one point in my young life, I even had my own room with a plastic tent that surrounded my bed, and only that doctor with the large finger could lift the side of this tent. Mom and Dad had to stay outside of this tent when visiting me. My memory is lost for how long of a hospital stay, living in that tent was, but it seems like weeks, if not months, along with the reason long gone of why I was placed in this clear plastic tent.

They are starting to build a new hospital, which would not have any nuns working there; the candy stripers would take their place for bedside care. I never did get any candy from anyone who wore those candy-striped outfits, but I did get better, and always was able to go home. That old hospital will always be forever sketched in my memories of all the little mishaps and unfortunate incidents that placed me inside as if I was a tenant.

This soon-to-be torn-down old hospital sits on top of a steep hill, where I have many painful memories of being held inside, like a jail cell keeping its prisoner trap. I only have a few memories from the outside of this old hospital. I can remember rolling down the steep grassy hillside, then over a bump, continuing rolling down the grassy hillside until you were so dizzy you could throw up. You always needed to stop before rolling onto a street or even rolling across the street, onto a stranger's front yard, that were at the bottom of the steep grassy hillside. I do remember this one trip there as Mom and Dad were visiting someone but cannot remember why. Mom and Dad went into the hospital, bringing items in a sack or bag, telling us it would only be for a little while, leaving that one older sister in charge of me and the two youngest siblings in Dad's parked car near the front of the hospital steps.

As soon as Mom and Dad were out of my sight, I jumped to the front seat of the car from the backseat. Now, I have never really gotten behind a steering wheel of a car before, and it seemed to be a good chance to do it now. There is an old saying it goes in one ear and out the other ear. For this is a true statement. I did not recall any warning that applied to me from our parents. With one leap of skill and balance over the car seat, with disapproval from that one older sister warning me, I start to play as though I am driving this car on a racetrack.

To sit behind a fine piece of modern-day engineering of quality craftsmanship automobile steering wheel released powerful energy. To put one's hands on this price and ignite a whimsical journey of travel is very intoxicating to a young child.

Dad's old car is a three-speed on the column, and just like Dad, I reached for this shinning metal handle, shifting into a high gear to win this imaginational race. A pull here, a push there, a mighty jerk freeing a once-locked gear shift handle, causing a loud bang, followed by backward movement of what was once a parked vehicle. While I started having this daydreaming fun, that one older sister was becoming a back-seat driver, not allowing my freedom from releasing me into this deep thought of racing, requesting that I stop playing with this quality, craftsmanship, automobile, mighty steering wheel.

Of course, this older sister is now threatening me that she will tell Mom and Dad when that loud bang happens, shocking me. I was amazed with the calculated skill of speed, with reaction time, plus distance displayed by that one older sister, with a leap of faith, easily clearing the front seat, pushing me out of the way, and implying eminence leg pressure to the brake, stopping this runaway car of Dad's, just before the low curb stop above that steep grassy hill side; possibly saving us children and stopping any property damage that could have happened. One must wonder how far this journey would have taken us with Dad's car in neutral, rolling down that steep grassy hillside. Could it be that Dad's car would have turned sideways and began rolling over and over all the way to the bottom, or perhaps even flipping end over end because of that large bump? If Dad's car would have remained on its wheels and continued to the bottom, it may have crashed into someone's house, coming to a rest in their front room. I guess that would have been one way of knowing what their house would look like from the inside.

Some adult stranger ran up to Dad's car and put it back into first gear, then applied the emergency brake. Oh, thanks to this one older sister for saving our lives, and sorry to the younger siblings for almost getting them killed. This adult stranger was heading into the hospital, but now was going to let Mom and Dad know that Dad's car is not properly parked correctly anymore outside in this hospital parking lot. What are the odds of this happening before this adult stranger can get into the hospital to inform Dad, the first people to come out of the hospital are Mom and Dad meeting this adult stranger on the steps? In some way, did these tattletale birds let my parents know they needed to come out? Did I mention there is a difference between a spanking and a whipping? I believe I may have gotten grounded, for life, from ever getting behind any steering wheel in a parked car or truck again.

Being grounded and getting sick makes it hard for a new kid to meet and make friends in this new town. I was supposed to start school before I started living in a tent at that old hospital. With school started, and leaving the hospital in the fall season, I did not get to meet many kids.

Needlessly to say, I still will be starting school late, and for the first time, away from Mom, not really knowing how to make new friends. We all know when a new kid starts school, there will be a picking order that follows. The larger and older kids pick on the younger kids; along with being a new kid, you will have a target on you. However, I do have a secret hidden weapon that all these other kids do not know about, and I plan to use it. When starting kindergarten back then, a child usually has one teacher, and this child only goes half-day to school, either in the morning or afternoon. My secret weapon is that one of the kindergarten teachers here at this school behind our home is my cousin. She is in her late thirties, possibly, and has been teaching for many years or so.

I have only met her a couple of times. Surely, I will have special treatment from a cousin. Quickly, my cousin, the teacher, denies my special treatment privileges on that very first day of school, along with meeting my cousin, the teacher, and her boss, the principal, who happens to know the family's home phone number. I often wonder what my parents thought about that first day school; within a few minutes of school starting, they would get a call from the boss of that school, the principal.

There is a difference between a spanking and whipping at home; moreover, teachers or principles would only do spankings at school until one becomes older. Of course, the child teacher would get the first swing on the chosen behind, then send or take the child to the principal's office. Then this child would get another spanking, followed by the phone call to your parents' home phone line. Oh, the pain! Oh, the hurt, when one gets home from school, and there is a difference between spanking and whipping. The parent high-court ruling did not matter if you received a spanking at school; what mattered is you are brought home for judgment of one's action while attending that school.

At all schools, the teachers would have their own paddles, but it seems the principal would have the best paddles. Teachers use yardsticks, rulers, fly swatters, and their bare hands, whereas the principal always had fine quality polish lumber, and one principal, I discovered years later, had a rubber hose attached to a wooden handle. I quickly learned that most teachers have tunnel vision and never see what happens first, only the reaction of a response. I thought of myself as good to depict a situation of what happened, but there are kids that are better at doing so. It was a day of firsts, and new for me: new school, new kids, possibly new friends, and even new shoes, pants, and shirts, along with a new playground to attend. This new school had classrooms upstairs, on three floors, classrooms on the main floor, and classrooms below the main floor. I went early so I could play in the playground, only to find out that when push comes to shove, one must shove back. Now, I had older siblings, so I did what little boys should do after a push and shove, I hit back just as the bell start to ring. This was the first time being with my cousin the teacher; she even held my hand, but not very gently, yanking me out of the school play yard, and into the school building.

Later, I learned all who had witnessed this event only saw me react to the pushing and shoves. So, I would start to plan my revenge, just like I do at home; planning a payback, for it was this bully's fault for having me introduced to a spanking at school. The plan would be simple: find a rock in the alley way or playground, hide it in my pocket, when one of the important subject is not looking, I will send it airmail to him. The playground is large and has some gravel in there too; you would think it be easy to find the right size, shape, and weight of a rock possibly there. The large playground is divided by a fence with swings, monkey bars, and a large slide inside the fence nearest the school. The lower part is a small baseball field with a backstop behind home plate. While the search continues for that perfect projectile rock, bigger kids will always pick on smaller kids, so the harassing continues. Within a few days, I do find the right projectile rock; now if I can get in the right position to airmail it.

I am not the only small kid that gets picked on in this playground; there are others. So, this plan of revenge will be for all the small kids in the playground and around the world; it is time to take a stand. Sometimes, when one does something that is possibly wrong but not for a selfish reason, it will not make it right, but it will not be as bad, moreover, then it becomes easier to do. I must be careful. If I get caught, I will get beat-up or spanked at school, worst yet, a spanking or whipping at home.

So, I am not even sure if I should go through with this daring plan of mine; after all, this kid may just stop picking on me. I cannot tell the teachers on the playground duty. I do not want to be labeled a tattletale like the birds I hate.

I still tell the teacher on duty, but she does not think much about it, just telling me I must try to get along with everyone. Here comes a slap in the back of the head from that bully child; so now there will be action. Again, a well-thought-out plan goes into effect as I maneuver myself around in the playground, closing the distance to the west, getting closure within my throwing range, hiding among the crowd like a hit man from the mafia gang.

A window of opportunity presents itself; hand in pocket, I retrieve this chosen rock, stepping into the throw, and release this projectile. Bart Star would have been proud of the accuracy of this projectile flight through the air as though angels guided it to impact. The projectile hits this bully kid right in the back of the head near the top. This toss was almost out of range. When this impact hits its target, the bell starts to ring, kids start to head back into the school as though they were trained animals getting into their lines. On this day, I was the first child in line and did not look back, making it all the way to the class-room, right to my desk, and started to color in my book, as my cousin, the teacher, got everyone else into their desks to begin our day of learning. My hands were shaking as I tried to color. I tried to relax.

There is noise in the classroom of children, but that big clock on the wall got to me. I could hear each second tick tock as though a loudspeaker was placed inside this clock. Seconds turned into one minute, and one-minute turns into two minutes; the shaking hand starts calm down. As I start to relax, an overwhelming feeling comes over me. I just scored one for all of us little kids. There will be sto-ries told of this day, in all the schools around the world. I will become famous. As the teachers start to ask questions about what we did before yesterday, my arm springs into action as a wave, like I am in a parade.

Wrong answer; some kids even laugh at me, but it did not matter to me. Not on this day! I did not even know what the question was. I have this hearing loss, and, some-times, I cannot hear the correct sentence the way it is told, or, sometimes, just a word or two will sound like a dif-ferent word. I went from such a scary moment; fear had me shaking, but as time passed, my fear changed to an incredible high; victory for us all! There was no bringing me down now. I was even listening to the teacher as best I could. I am in the clear; this mission is a successful success. Then a thundering pounding that rattled the window on the classroom door, making everyone in the class look back at this door. In walked the principal herself, apologizing for disrupting this teacher's class, although she needs one of these students to come with her.

As my name escapes the principal's lips, coming from her inner being, as in slow motion, echoing in the classroom with the sound of monition, much louder than the tick tock a little while ago, now all heads have turned and look at me. The teacher asked if I would be coming back? "Not today," was a response by the principal. The teacher asked me to put away my things and go with the principal. I want to say, "No, I do not want to go," but I knew the best strategy now was to say nothing at all. I neatly put away my things, get up and walk, with everyone looking at me, toward the principal as she thanks the teacher.

We walk in silence toward her office upstairs; when we get to the principal's office, she has me sit down in this large brown chair. I wait there in a moment of silence till she asked, "What do you have to say about what happened?" "Nothing. I do not know what you are talking about," I replied with that innocent little boy voice and look.

Just then, a bird lands on her office windowsill and sits there for a few seconds, looking at me through the open window, right into my eyes, making cooing sounds while sitting there. We both had turned our heads to watch this bird, and then this bird turns its head to look at me for a few seconds, tilting its head side to side before looking back at the principle, and starts to make more cooing sounds, then we watch this bird fly away, turning our heads back to looking at each other. "That is the very same bird that came here earlier and told me that you threw a rock, hitting another student in the back of the head," this principal state; there possibly could have been a grin upon her lips.

As each word settled into my being, I lost all my strength, my ability to answer and to move; all I could do was shake my head in response to additionally questioning. I am shocked; how dare these creatures of Mother Nature bird's tattletale on me, knowing that I was not doing anything wrong. Why did that tattletale bird not tattletale on that bully boy that was hitting me, and what he had done before? An imminent power starts to energize deep within me and build strength. Pow! It hits and gives me speaking power. "What did this bird tell you about what that bully did?" I questioned the principal.

I did not get spanked from that principal on this day. I just waited in silence until Mom would arrive to escort me home. There was no need to explain my actions on this day. I tried, but no one would believe me over these tattletale birds. Even at home, my pleas of what happened could not be heard, listening with false ears, not wanting to know the truth. There is a difference between spanking and whipping; oh, the pain! Oh, it hurt; again, caused by lies from tattletale birds; oh, yes, sorry about that to this bully boy that I hit with a rock. I should have not done that.

These devil tattletale birds have gone too far; they have no rules, no boundaries, and they will tell anyone that can listen to them and will do so until I stop them! I now know these evil tattletale birds will tell all adults, and I believe all adults can communicate with these mean tattletale birds. It would be a couple of weeks before I am free from my home; I am a prisoner again, not allowed to play outside, not even in the yard. I had a couple of weeks planning on what I should do to these devil creatures, now that I knew for sure that they were here in this town, against me.

Their mouths are big and filled with only lies, not telling the complete story of what happened, for they choose to pick only on me. One good thing about having an alleyway between our home and the school is there are lots of rocks; lots of ammo. If only I had my slingshot. I do wonder if we brought it here when we moved to this new home. Were there extra slingshots made, forgotten, and misplaced? There are many things that can happen in a move; you lose items, and you find items that were lost.

As in my case, while I am searching in our old store building storage facility, looking for my missing slingshot, I find items that I did not know we had. Then I came across animal traps of different sizes and shapes. I wonder if dad used to be a trapper, just like the mountain men. Wow, this is too cool; my dad was a mountain man, a trapper; if only he could instruct me on catching a tattletale bird, then I could teach this tattletale bird a lesson.

As I start to examine these traps, some are just too large to use. I cannot open them; they must be used on bears or lions. Others have too sharp of an edge, but I can possibly still use them. Some are made of hard wire, shaped in a square, not oval shape, as most are. First and foremost, I must hide some of these traps, just in case, and I hide a square one and a couple of smaller jaw ones in another room.

I start to figure out how some of these traps work, how to use them; it is not hard; simple mechanic engineering. You must pry open the smaller traps, then using a lever notching it into place, holding the trap open. Then the animal must step into this trap, releasing the lever-locking notch, which will snap the jaws closed. Some of these traps are too hard to press open to latch, forcing me to work on the smaller traps. After setting a couple into the open position, I use a yardstick to set the trap off. Bingo. I got this figured out. This is so awesomely cool; the trap will jump into the air as it is clamping its jaws close onto the yardstick, a few inches up from the floor. I did not know that these traps would do this—jump up like that—but now it makes sense of this movement; it will only increase your chances in trapping something. My younger brother comes in, and his eyes light up, he is just as surprised and excited as I am about this new discovery.

I start to explain the use of these traps as though I am an expert trapper to my younger brother, even having him set some of the smaller traps up with little to no help from me. Like the glow from a full moon, the light lets you see in the dark, and now this glow starts to develop an idea deep inside my brain. "Hey, we can take turns setting up some traps in the backyard, and then we can take turns trying to find them," I told my younger brother. "We will know who is better at hiding and finding the traps." We will use these yardsticks to find the traps that we hide in the dirt," I said to him. He thought this was a good idea as well as we decide on which traps to use. The smaller traps seemed to be the best to use because my younger brother could set them easier. These traps were most likely used to catch smaller animals, such as bobcats, foxes, and coyotes.

We chose three of the smaller traps, and then hid them under our shirts. I grab the yardstick, and we head to the backyard. With these chickens being penned up, we could play in the side and backyard. During the move, we did bring the chickens to this new home of ours, and they have a chicken coop in the backyard made from an old attached shed to that old store we used for storage. Although there was a law about having chickens in the city limits, nobody said anything about them, and I cannot recall what the law stated. We did, however, have a new red rooster named Elmer, and Elmer is not afraid of anything; he only respects our dad. You did not mess around with Elmer, who is very mean and dangerous, and will attack anyone if Elmer is out of the pen. Elmer even had his own pen under the kitchen porch.

Dad would put Elmer under the kitchen porch so the collection of eggs could be had, and we always had fresh eggs. If Mom decided on chicken for dinner, she would have Dad go get dinner in the yard. I was amazed at how the chickens would hold still as Dad would place the chickens' heads and neck on the chopping block of wood, just holding them by their legs. Then with one swift swing of his sharp hatchet, he removed the chicken's head, or, sometimes, Dad would cut on the side of the chicken head behind the ear with a sharp knife; we knew we were having chicken for dinner. Yes, chickens can and do walk for a little while without nothing attached to the top of their necks. On this day, the backyard belonged to us children, for our venture waited for this great game of dare, finding loaded ready steel animal traps!

This plan would be simple: we would stay close to the oak tree in the backyard and could use the fallen leaves and loose dirt to cover these animal traps. This hiding area would be more than ten square feet. My younger brother won the right to hide these animal traps first, and then I would use the yardstick in search of these loaded daring animal traps. Yes, it was a game of dare and yes; if you failed in finding these animal traps hidden in the dirt covered with leaves, it may result in bodily injury.

If one is not good at finding things, one may step into one of these animal traps with one's foot, possibly losing a toe or two! Even in setting these animal traps, one can slip and lose a finger or two! Of course, we did not think of the results of possibly danger if we failed on what type of injury we could end up with. I left the yardstick with my younger brother as he left to hides these animal traps in the side and backyard behind this wooden gate with attached chicken wire. I would wait in the front yard for him to come and get me. The wait seemed long in anticipation of this great challenge that awaited me to succeed in finding these animal traps. Failure would only be painful to the one that stepped onto any one of these animal traps. Here came my younger brother; time had come to start this great game of dare!

We opened the wood gate again and went into the side and backyard. The chickens were quiet as we passed the chicken coop, heading to the northwest corner of the backyard, to the oak tree. I saw the yardstick, grabbed it, and started to overlook the area to see if there were any easy sightings of these hidden animal traps.

Like a skilled trapper, I maneuvered carefully through the area till I spotted one trap, and in less of a second, I sprang this animal trap with the jaws closing with a mighty snap; one down. I removed the animal trap from the yardstick; by stepping on it, it loosens the steel jaws to free the yardstick. I saw another one and thought about using the tip of my shoe to uncover this animal trap; *better not try that*, I thought to myself. Now, using the yardstick, I sprang the second trap jaws of death. Two down, and then the last one is spotted. I sprang this trap with amazing skill. Now, it was my turn to hide these three animal traps for my younger brother to find them!

I sent my younger brother to the front yard to wait so I could hide these animal traps. He did not do a bad job of hiding these animal traps; however, I must do much better in hiding these animal traps if I was going to win this game of dare. As I watched my younger brother leave, going past the wooden gate to the front yard, my plan was ready to go. I would set these animal traps as I laid them down to see how they would be hidden. I would leave just one animal trap kind of hidden near the oak tree so he could spot it, leaving the other two very well-hidden animal traps in the pathway. This decoy animal trap should lure my younger brother right over the very well-hidden animal traps. I did not want to make it too hard on him, but hard enough to win this game of dare! I piled extra leaves on these two animal traps in this pathway. Then, in this same area where there were no animal traps hidden, I made more piles of leaves, making them look like animal traps were hidden there. I stood back, overlooking the area to make sure there were no exposed traps or chains. These chains were attached to these traps, then the chains could be attached to trees and roots, or spike down into the soil, capturing the animal to keep it from leaving. I was ready; it looked like I would win this game of dare; everything was well hidden as I turned to go get my younger brother waiting in the front yard. I called to my younger brother that I was ready—if he was ready to go and search for these animal traps! Without hesitation, he turned and headed toward the backyard with all the confidence of a skilled trapper.

He grabbed for the yardstick and then started to cheat, using it like a broom. I told him, "That is not fair; you cannot use the yardstick as a broom. You can only go up and down with the yardstick." After we go over the rules that we came up with, my younger brother had extraordinarily little trouble finding the hidden animal traps. I am shocked. I underestimated his ability in locating these traps; time for round two. I left the backyard so he could hide these animal traps as I waited in the front yard. I started to come up with a much better plan on how to hide these animal traps.

My younger brother hollers at me from the backyard from behind that wooden gate, to come look for these animal traps. My turn of dare has come again as I turn to head into the backyard. When I get to the backyard, I reach for the yardstick, but did not see any signs of hidden animal traps. My younger brother did a much better job this time as I look over the area. I spot one hidden deep into the soil, so I carefully move over to release the jaws of pain and drop the yardstick hard in it, snapping the speeding jaws closed, cutting the bottom end of the yardstick cleanly off; awesome power, what a rush of excitement. The yardstick must have gotten weak from the closing jaws of death from these animal traps. This was the first time it cut through the yardstick. I set off another trap, and again, the jaws of pain cut through the yardstick. Wow, this was so cool. I told my younger brother that I would use this end that got cut off and he would use the other end of the yardstick. I find the last animal trap, drop in the yardstick, and set it off. This animal trap clamped

72

up into a new area on the yardstick, making an indention on the yardstick. It was his turn to go and wait for me to re-hide these animal traps, as I would put my new plan into action hiding these animal traps.

I dig three holes deep enough so that these animal traps would step inside and flush with the soil around them. Then I set these animal traps, placing them inside these holes, carefully filling with dirt in and around them all, covering them all over. The only thing next to exposing these animal traps is the centerpiece. I find just one large leaf and place it over the centerpiece, covering it. I do this with the other two remaining animal traps. I avoid these traps as I set up decoys of traps that may be there, using dirt and leaves, being careful not to touch the three real traps in front of all these decoys. I make sure every leaf is in its place and turn to go get my younger brother. This time, as I neared the wooden gate with the chicken wire on it, two birds sitting on top of this gate start flying off. Dang, if I were paying attention better, I could have thrown a rock or something at these two birds. Now, I call out to my younger brother, for it is his turn of dare.

As we head toward the oak tree in the backyard where the animal traps are hidden, something starts to stir in my brain. My younger brother grabs the yardstick, and just like a lightning bolt, this idea comes to life. I tell my younger brother to start to look for these animal traps without me, as I head back into this storage building. I am going to change this game of dare between my younger brother and I, placing it on these tattletale birds.

I start to look for the chicken feed; this is going to end the war of tattletale birds forever. Why didn't I think of this before? With this new plan of mine, I will sprinkle in the middle of a set trap some chickenfeed. Let those tattle-tale birds come back for this chickenfeed with their beaks pecking, setting off one of these animal traps, perhaps chopping off their head. Now, where did I put that chicken seed earlier when I was hiding these two other traps?

After searching for a while, I remember the chicken-feed is by the door that I just came through. I do not need a lot of feed, just a handful will do. I look for a small container, but I cannot find one, so instead, I will use a metal coffee can and put some chickenfeed in it. I got the chickenfeed, and out the door I go with a smile as big as a mountain range to the West.

As I step outside the storage door, there is Dad, going up the kitchen steps toward the kitchen door, towing my younger brother along by his ear. I wonder how my younger brother got into trouble as I jump back into this storage building.

There is no time to waste as they go into the kitchen door, then I head toward the backyard. When I get to the backyard, I see my younger brother did find all three animal traps; as I get ready to set the first animal trap up, I hear that sound every little boy dreaded to hear. I wonder why my parents are calling me. I have not done anything wrong as far as I know.

Oh, the pain! Oh, the hurt! Have I mentioned there is a difference between these spankings and a whipping? Needlessly to say, I am again a home prisoner, grounded for life in the use of these animal traps. All traps were removed and hidden somewhere else. All these devil tattletale birds; I do truly hate them. After learning about the possible of injuries from these animal traps and the game of dare from our parents, I did not think our parents understood what the game of dare was all about. Yes, we could have lost a finger or all of them, along with possibly a broken hand or wrist on our upper extremes. Just as dangerous was the possibility of losing a toe or two, possibly all of them, along with a broken foot on the lower extremity, but that is the dare part of this game. We did succeed in the dare part of the game before we were stopped from playing it. A child's mind sometimes is just that, a child's mind. However, the fact remains this battle was won again by tattletale birds, and the war will continue.

I am allowed freedom again from the home prison after a couple of weeks, and I still owe my younger brother the payback; he broke during his spanking, and let our parents know I was there with him on the settings of these animal traps. I still kind of do not want to play with my younger brother as he asked me to play with trucks with him in the backyard. I tell him, "What for? So, you can tell on me again?" The war of tattletale birds weighed heavily on me as I tried to come up with another plan. I just do not feel like playing right now. An imminent power starts to energize deep within me and build strength. Pow! Another great idea just burst into the scene of my mind. This idea is not about the tattletale birds; it is about payback on my younger brother. I have been in a front yard for a while when this idea creates different alternatives with quick action, since it will work right about now. My younger brother will be in the backyard playing with his trucks. I sneak through the wooden gate, open it quietly, and to where Elmer's pen is under the porch. I open the pen door slightly, run back, and close the wooden gate behind me as a bird flies just above my head as though it was going to land and eat some of the chickenfeed left by the chickens on the ground.

Elmer kicks open the door to his pen, coming out like a racehorse out of the gates for race. He runs right toward the wooden gate, all the time, making sure I am behind the chicken wire. He stretches around for a second or two, then realizes someone is in his territory. Elmar turns and moves over to look further toward the backyard. Yep, he is off running like the Roadrunner in the coyote cartoons. The screams have started becoming horrific, terrifying, and extremely loud as the attack of Elmer is on, but some of the screams are not from my younger brother.

Perhaps I should have looked in the backyard first before letting Elmer, this crazy rooster, out of his pen. We do have a side door to the backyard, so when Mom went out to hang the clothes to dry, I did not see her there.

Sorry, ma'am for that. I did not know you were hanging clothes in the yard at that very moment. Sorry, younger brother. I should not have let Elmer out to assault you. I had the lowest feeling many times as a child, but this time, my heart is broken, as I really feel bad, for Moms' legs were all scratched up and pecked up by Elmer. Mom used the clean clothes to fight off this rooster named Elmer before Dad heard the screams, coming out to stop the assault on both Mom and my younger brother. Of course, she has to re-wash the clothes, since they fell out of the basket.

How did our parents find out so quickly, with shocking speed, that I was the one releasing hell on my mom and younger brother by setting free this derange rooster name Elmer? It had to be that one bird that flew over my head when trying to get some chickenfeed. I will never know for sure, but I think these tattletale birds can tell on me right away without waiting or, perhaps, can understand the outcome of my actions before I can, and let my parents or adults know.

The judgment was swift; oh, the pain, oh the hurt; have I mentioned there is a difference between a spanking and whipping? I am again a prisoner of my own home. I am starting to really dislike these spankings, along with the grounding punishments I keep receiving. I did not even get to watch the first-aid training done by Dad, on Mom's legs I wonder if Dad had a grin upon his lips, and the first-aid training Dad did on my younger brother's back, neck, and head.

The cold shoulder Mom gave me for the next few days was worse than any other punishment I got before. Mom's answers were quick and mostly one word after all my questions. "No" was her favorite reply, and sometimes, "What do you think?" I was once your favorite beloved son; now, just a brat; back to be my dad's son. I cannot believe these tattletale birds broke my bond between my mom and I; these mean tattletale birds will pay for this dearly. Mom will instill in me, throughout my life, how to forgive, and after a few days, she forgave me for my carelessness actions. I am back into Mom's presence, back into her glow, almost back to be her favorite beloved child. Oh, but these tattletale birds must pay for this heartbreak they put me through, and I will get my chance one day to redeem myself.

Once again, I am free from my home prison, and as fate would have it, I come across a great new idea, thanks to Mother Nature herself. As I watch the chickens eat their feed in the backyard through the wooden gate chicken wire, some birds land and try to feed with the chickens. The chickens did not mind sharing their feed with these birds: however, Elmer did get offended. Every time a bird would land in the feeding area, Elmer was quick to chase them away. If only Elmer could fly, he could catch those tattletale birds, but Dad cuts all the chickens' wings feathers, so they could not fly away. Just like a storm that starts above the ocean water circulating, and starts to become larger, building strength till it become a full-blown hurricane, my thoughts deep inside my brain start to circle around, forming together into full strength an idea of a great plan that may not fail. This plan will work in ending this war, once and for all, against these tattle-tale birds. How did I not think of this before? Now, we had lots of pets: chickens, rabbits, ducks, dogs, and even Shetland ponies; however, we never had a pet cat that I could recall. Dogs do not like cats, and cats are natural enemies of birds, so quickly I go inside the home in search of my parents.

After many tries for permission to get a pet cat, both Mom and Dad decline me, with Dad finally stating, "Don't ask again." Why we could not have a pet cat I cannot remember why, and we never did get a pet cat. If I cannot have a pet cat of my own, then I will have to borrow a cat from the neighborhood, and I have seen plenty of cats around the house.

Now, how does one go about catching a cat, then train this old captured cat to capture and eat tattletale birds? If I catch a cat and hold this cat without food for a day or so, and while the chickens are penned up, I could scatter chickenfeed around to lure these tattletale birds in the yard. Then, release this hungry cat, and behold, the sight of capture, and death of a tattletale bird. Mother Nature against Mother Nature, and the victory will be mine.

This cat will be rewarded with nothing but the best of food for the rest of its life. What kind of food can I use to catch a cat since we do not have any cat food? However, we do have lots of cans of tuna. I even like to eat tuna, and tuna will work simply fine, but what to use for capturing? After all, I still have two traps hidden; could they possibly work? One small trap with the sharp edge will not work, remembering what happened to the yardstick being sliced off into two pieces. I do not want to cut off a cat's leg, or worse, the cat's head off. One trap is made of out of heavy gauge wire; it may just work fine for this plan. Now, as I see it, it would be better to catch a cat at night, since at night is when I have heard cats. Sometimes, by our trash cans, the cats would meow. This will be perfect since we have this door on the west of the house leading to the side and backyard.

This house that we moved into has four entry doors. The first entry door is in the front of the house going into the living room. The second entry door is about twenty feet back, and this entry door heads into the kitchen. We have an entry door in the boys' bedroom that leads to the side, backyard, and alleyway. The last entry door is in the attached garage in the back of the house. I think it would be best to set the trap in the dark, and I would have a back-porch light to turn on, to see what I am doing. I sneak a can of tuna out of the pantry, hiding it in our bedroom along with my Army can opener. Now, to get the hardwired trap out of storage building without getting caught with the duct tape, a tent spike, a hammer, and a five-gallon bucket with a lid. I will make small air holes in this five-gallon bucket lid. The spike, hammer, duct tape, and a five-gallon bucket with a lid are easy to find. I had little trouble finding a tent stake to nail down the trap but found a gutter spike to use for the traps. One by one, I get what I need, hiding them in our room except for the bucket, of course; it was too big to hide, so I hid this bucket in the backyard, and then made holes in the lid. The plan is almost ready to go into effect; let the battles begin, with Mother Nature against Mother Nature soon to happen.

I sneak out at night and pound the spike through the loop on the chain attached to the trap, securing the trap from being ripped away. Then I tape the small stick onto the trap. I do not want to break a foot, leg, or, worse yet, the cat's neck. The stick will keep the trap from closing all the way, but still should hold the cat in the trap. All that was left was to open the tuna and place some on the ground, then set the trap up near the tuna. I set the trap near the wall so the cat can only come from three directions. I am proud with the results; I did put a lot of thought into this plan. I have a five-gallon bucket lid with holes in it to place on top of the bucket that will soon hold a captured cat. Now, all I must do is wait inside the bedroom and, hopefully, I could hear the trap being released. The waiting turns into boredom, with no results at all, and now it is bedtime. As my two brothers and I go to bed, I start to plan some more.

Maybe I should try a chickenfeed in that one small trap that I have hidden. Then I fall asleep, only to wake up in that place where you are half asleep with being half awake.

"It is La Llorona!" my younger brother cries out, as I come to a complete startled awareness. Outside in the backyard are screams of terror. I jump out of bed, put on my slippers, and say it is a catfight. I turn on the porch light and race out the side door into the backyard, where I see this captured cat. This cat has the chain on the trap stretched tight as this cat is desperately trying to free itself with yanks, jumps, and twists, as I move over to a better place to grab this cat. This cat turns and attacks me. I jumped back, narrowly escaping the claws that reached out to scratch out my eyes. Well, this cat is in the air somehow it pulled out its paw from the trap, landing on the ground on all four paws.

The cat looks me in the eye, turns, and runs to the trash can, jumps on top of it, then jumps over the fence and runs into the darkness.

"Wow," I say, "did you see how mad that cat was?" as I am turning around, then I see not only my two brothers but also Dad standing there in the doorway. "What a cat-fight," I say, not knowing what to do next. Dad states, "That is enough; get in the house," as I start walking back to the door. I am wondering what exactly Dad witnessed. Once I am in the bedroom, Dad just tells us to get back into bed and go to sleep. As I am in lying in bed, waiting for more to come from Dad, but nothing happens. That cat was mad as holy, and I did not plan on that cat attacking me. Oh, by the way, sorry, cat. I should have not tried to trap you. I wonder how trappers get the trapped animals out of their traps. That is when it hits me; I better hide all the material in the morning so I will not get caught for trapping this cat. When morning came, I did the job of taking apart the trap and returning it to its hiding place, just in case I would need it again. I do this with ease, leaving only the bucket with the lid. Then the waiting game comes. I know, sooner or later, I will get the news about the trap capturing a cat along with the whippings that are about to come. Time moves so slowly that day, as I waited, but no one ever came to call me in that Dad or Mom wanted to speak to me. The night came and went, and just like that, the next day came, then the night, then the third day came and went. That is when it hit me; these tattletale birds could not tell on me because they were asleep.

Yes, birds sleep at night; they did not see what happened. This must be the reason why they did not say

80

anything to my parents! This will change everything now that I have learned about these tattletale birds. Although this was not a victory in this battle in the war of the tattle-tale birds, the information that came to be known to me would one day help me end this war. This now explained why I hardly got into trouble at night. I knew I could use this information, and I would learn different and better battling plans. I have been in war now, which seems like many years, but victory was again within my grasp. I hated tattletale birds!

By Robert J.

DEATH OF A TATTLETALE BIRD

CHAPTER 4

Some of these old photos bring joyful, heartfelt, and sorrowful memories, as I continue to turn pages in this old photo album. It seems so long ago that I was a young child living in these photos, but in all reality, it is only a moment ago, and time keeps moving along. As a family, we took lots of rides looking at all of Mother Nature's beauty around us, even all wildlife. Many photos of wildlife, like this one photo of a suspended red tail hawk in flight, felt like it happened only yesterday, capturing this red tail hawk on film.

In a child's eye, life moves slowly, like this red tail hawk, gliding in the wind. This red tail hawk spreads out its wings, capturing the unseen breeze, floating in air as though there is an invisible string from the heavens above, suspending it in that moment; only moving with its choice so gracefully, without visible movements, at times, from its wings or tail feathers. This red tail hawk can move up, down, forward, and backward, or magically staying in place. As time continues to move all around this red tail hawk, like a large rock in a small river, it stays in place as water continues to flow by. This red tail hawk just floats there as time passes around it; moreover, just waiting for its time to move on. Like all young children, times move slowly, and everyone over thirty is old.

As a child, you can hardly wait for Christmas to arrive, and then after it hits you, it takes another year for it to return. If you did not get what you wanted, you could only hope it will arrive on your birthday or wait that exceptionally long year to pass. My birthday was at the end of summer, and just like Christmas, it would take forever to get here. We all know, as children, the closer to the end of the school year, time moves slower. For some children, the wait for the school year to start moves just as slowly. However, the summer break just flies by, and before you know it, the school year has started again. Time waits for no one, and it continues to move on, and before you know it, an opportune time has passed.

I flipped a few other pages in that old photo album. Looking at photos captured in time past, it is like that red tail hawk that floats back or forward, without changing height, and sometimes floating out of sight. This one photo I am looking at, I am holding an object in my left hand, and as I look closer at this object, my mind floats back to this captured time past, and, once again, I am living in my thoughts. I am older, and with age, comes experience, along with knowledge, yet I am still trying to win just one battle with these tattletale birds.

I came up with a plan to catch one tattletale bird at night while they slept, while sleeping in my bed. This plan came together in my dreams, flowing into my brain. This plan would include a long stick, duct tape, and fishing net on the end of that long stick. All I would need to do would be to climb up the oak tree in the backyard at night and net a tattletale bird, and then put it in a cage. Victory, then, would be mine! I slowly learned it is ridiculously hard to climb a tree in the dark, way up to the upper branches where these tattletale birds roost, and when a plan falls apart, so does a boy fall from that oak tree. Oh, the pain! Oh, the hurt! Another first-aid training class on how to splint a broken arm, and there could have been a grin on Dad's lips.

I end up with another visit to that large-finger doctor in the new hospital, along with another cast on my arm. I think I saw a grin on that large-finger doctor's lips. Why can I not win just one battle? I feel like I failed everyone who the tattletale birds pick on. And why do birds not sleep at night? Why do tattletale birds pick mostly on me? Yes, depression can happen to a young child, and I am very depressed again. The only one good thing that came out of the failed tree-climbing plan was that the tattletale birds did not tattletale on me. Why did they not tell? Even with a broken arm, I was able to throw the stick with the fishing net onto the roof of the shed. Yet, my parents believed that my mental capabilities were not functioning normally again; why else would I be climbing a tree at night? Like all parents at that time, they believed that idle hands were the devil's workshop. So, now, more chores are placed upon me as the cast is removed, and I even end up with some small jobs around the neighborhood.

I never did get allowance from our parents, so by doing these little jobs, I end up with some cash. I could not believe it, at first, that people would pay me to cut their grass and pull their weeds. I have done this for free many times as a punishment for my failure to understand such rules that apply for me to follow. This is my first job that put money in my pockets, and got me out of that depressed state I was in. I started to save money so I could buy a new bike, like one that you could shift gears, and cool hand brakes on the high chrome handlebars with a banana seat. I almost forgot about that tattletale bird war because I was so busy. Then came one day, when my parents were going downtown to shop at a non-grocery store, and I wanted to go with them.

I would hate going grocery-store shopping with our parents; they were so slow, going up and down every aisle, looking at different items and prices. Now, on this day, they were headed downtown to a national chain store; there, I could find out how much money it would take to buy the bike I liked. The store was large, with a main floor and a full basement, and sold everything you wanted or needed. The family would get these big catalogs in the mail where you could buy everything, just like the store we were headed to. When we got there, I headed downstairs, trying to keep from running to where the sporting goods section was.

Oh, they had some fine-looking bikes there, and just the one I wanted was displayed so proudly, so majestically that I could not take my eyes off it! High chrome handlebar with black-hand brakes along with a white banana seat, on a bright green frame and bright red full reflectors, and this bike was a five-speed! This bike looked like it could fly; this was the one I wanted so badly! But then I went into a shock, looking at the price tag, and quickly learned I would have to work a lifetime to afford a bike like this. All the air in me just drained out as though a vacuum hose was attached to my lungs; they cost so much money. This was like Christmas time when you did not get that one present you longed for so much. I started to move down the aisles, like a zombie wondering around, lost in my own world, just looking around in a daze state, when this dark figure display caught my eye.

This dark display showed a black stock pump BB gun, this black glow was for me as though it was calling to me, "Come buy me." I could not see the price tag, so I asked a worker there how much this BB gun would cost. The worker grabbed a box below the counter and looked at it and gave me the price of this black gold weapon. I asked how much a box of BB pellets cost would. Immediately, I knew I would have enough money with my next two or three completed yard jobs to purchase this fine American-made professional weapon. I was so excited I ran upstairs from the counter, looking for my parents. Then this image hit me of Mom and Dad shaking their head from left to right; no!

Mom and Dad may not like the idea of me possessing an American-made professional weapon. I better butter them up first, making sure that I am my mom's son, and everything is good.

After finding Mom and Dad upstairs, I quickly explained that we needed to go home because I was tired of shopping already. I needed to get home and go do the next couple of yards so I could get paid so I could ride my old bike back downtown to purchase this beautiful American-made professional weapon. Mom and Dad were not in any hurry to leave this store, so no matter how much whining I did, until the threat of being grounded did I close my mouth. What seemed like a month in the store, Dad and Mom finally made their purchase after numerous talks with the salesperson, and we could leave and go home.

Quickly, I went and did the next job on my list, borrowing our own lawn mower to complete it, making sure I even raked. I even picked up trash so that the yard looked very nice; this might have been my best job ever. Now, I counted the money, and I did not have enough money to purchase this American-made professional weapon of a BB gun, along with BBs. Then I remembered my friend's older brother saying that at church, you can get free money if your hands were fast enough.

This tale told to me seemed too good to be true; perhaps this person was trying to trick us into getting into trouble. As he explained, while he was at church, they bring out these baskets with long handles, passing them in front of people who would put money in these baskets. The rule is that while the basket comes by, you can put money into it or hit it up sending the money out of the basket. Any money you catch in the air is yours to keep, only if the valve is greater than money that falls out and lands on the pew and floor. All this money that landed on the pew and floor must go back into the basket after the basket holder counts it. If the valve of the money you catch in the air is greater, then you get to keep what you caught. Now, if yours is less in valve than what was on the pew and floor, then it must all go back into the basket and you will lose your chance, never to try again. I have been to church, and yes, there are these baskets that come by. I, myself, have put dollars that Dad or Mom gave us to put in these baskets.

This older child states that there was one older gentleman who did catch more money in the air than what fell on the pew and floor, and everyone in church cheer and clapped, and as far as this child knew, no child has ever tried this feat. There is a twist to this story; that basket holder does not have to let you try and can yank back the basket away from your attempt. Sometimes, as a young child, my sensible sense will not awaken with me in the mornings, so I just stay in bed, leaving me to face the day alone.

After we had moved to this town, I started to attend a church that would teach children about God. Mostly, at first, I would stay with Mom in the church, sitting on pews, listening to a preacher speak about God and Jesus. As I grew older, I would attend church school as my parents attended church. The nuns would teach us about these Bible stories. I wanted my mom to be proud of her son in the way he would listen to these stories. One day, there was a little party for us kids that attended these classes; as I was managing my good behavior skills, when a nun placed a cookie in my plate, I thanked her with the common answer back then, "Thank you, ma'am." This nun turns back to me and slaps me in the face, and then this nun states, "You call me 'Sister.' I am your sister." I was a biter when I was young; I guess that was my way to express myself. I had trouble pronouncing many words, so I would express myself differently at times. Sorry to that nun; maybe I should not bite anyone.

I was not allowed back to church school for a while but did return to those classes; I wonder if it was all the praying from my mom. I even did make my first communion in that same church, although I was in a wheelchair at that time with a broken right leg. Now, we attend the largest church in town with the closing of that smaller church, as I ponder this information of quick hands. Could this possibly be true, hitting these baskets up send money floating in the air, to grab before the money descends back toward the benches and floor? Do I have the skill set to accomplish this feat since no child has even tried to do this? As good as this tale sounds, I am going to have to pass. I am too close to have all the money saved up; moreover, I do play jacks a lot more now, training to catch things in the air.

Now, as I sit on these pews, I wonder if it is possible as I eye out the basket coming toward us. Dad has many rules about many things, like to drop the dollar in the basket from above the basket; you do not reach into the basket to leave money. If things sound too good to be real, then they are not real. This is an elderly man on the basket handle, coming toward us, and his skill is rather slow in moving the basket to each person. An imminent power starts to energize deep within me and build strength. Pow! It hits. The whacking noise echoes throughout the cathedral ceiling; everyone jumps and turns simultaneously, looking toward what made the noise. The items in the basket float slowly in the air, daring me to grab it all; however, as I reach for the items that look like dollar bills, something just stops me, for reasons of unknown to me, on why I should not take these bills. All items then suddenly drop from the air to the pews and floor. Then I feel all eyes on me. I do not think that I will ever see so many shocked reactions on all faces again in my lifetime. And it is awfully hard to catch flying money in the air; it goes everywhere, along with small envelopes that were in the basket. I was the center of attention for that moment in church, and it weighed heavily on me. When we left that church on this day, pigeons were all over outside and flew up noisily as Mom and Dad hustled us out of church. I think these pigeons are laughing at me! I do not remember if the complete family got banned from this church, or if I was the only one banned for a while. Sorry, family, for that was a mistake I made.

Prison time in the new house seemed to move just as slowly as the old home did, and I am only allowed to do my choirs and the yards people hired me to do. With my freedom comes the knowing that I am still short from my great purchase. I start to collect cans and bottles all around the neighborhood, and now, finally, I had enough money. How do I sneak away to make such a purchase, and I do know of taxes, but how much did these taxes add up to? But I should have enough money to cover them, and I feel like an adult. I have worked for everything I am about to get very soon. I will have what it takes to end this war, once for all. I am sick of tattletale birds laughing at me, telling on me.

Our neighbor son has a pump BB gun, and he has shown us how they work and the accuracy of the BBs; how to load such weapons, and what oil is best for the barrel. This friend states that the more pumps on this BB gun, the greater the distance, even up to the park one block away. Everything is coming together, for now, I think this is a blessing that God has given me; the drive to work hard, knowing that the money I saved up would really be for a weapon to end this war and not a new bike for me. Children from around the world will be talking about me and all the hard work I did for all of us children.

I put on nice clean clothes, get all my money, add rope to my bike seat, and I ride downtown. I chain up my bike and walk into this business like I am the owner. Downstairs, I travel, and right to the counter, asking a salesman about this weapon. This salesman asked me how old I am, and I lie to him while breaking out very cold hard cash.

I ask for a small box of BBs, and the salesman asks if I need oil for the barrel. I shake my head no, then I make the purchase. I slowly start to walk away from the counter when the salesman states, "Do not forget to put a couple of drops of oil in the barrel." I nod my head, turn around to walk out of the store, only to pick up my pace, trying not to run out of this store. Outside, I unlock my bike, put BB pellets box in my pocket, balance out the BB gun box in my arm, and start to ride home.

I have the power of ten men in my legs. I am a bad*** as I petal toward home. People driving by in their cars are waving, giving thumbs-up signals. I imagine children in the cars are cheering for me! The warmth of the sun heats up my being; the breeze in the air blows so gently across my face as I near our home. Now, one must become a Indian brave to sneak into the house through that side door, hoping Elmer is penned up. Just my luck, the chickens are penned up as I quickly head toward this side door. Robins fly up from behind the trashcans, giving me a fright that stops my heart.

The door is locked. I must put down the BB gun box behind the trashcan so no one will see it and go inside to open the side door. I pass through the house like a ghost on Halloween not getting noticed and make way to our shared bedroom. With no one in sight, I go get my treasure and hide it under my bed. Then, quickly, I leave my room and head outdoors to get my bike. I ride to the park one block away and play at the playground. I have done the impossible. I am sky high; nothing can bring me down. I think about trying to swing over the top crossbar on the swing set, but friends ride up to play. I tell them about my amazing stories, but they do not believe me. We all ride over to the alleyway behind my home, and I ask them to wait there. I ride to the front of the house and go in to drink some water and check what is on TV, then I head toward my bedroom. With no one around, I get the BB gun box out and head out that side door.

I show my friends this marvel gift I gave myself; all my friends want to shoot it right now, but I say "no." I cannot do that now. I must put it away for later. Some of my friends say they are going home to get their money and go buy a BB gun at that store. Just before my friends take off, one friend shouts out, "Look at the birds in the tree; we could shoot them," This one bird stares me down, eye to eye. I can see this bird's pupil as though I am looking through binoculars. I turn and head inside to hide my treasure again under my bed, then to the front room to watch TV. I am the king of the house. I will be the hero kid of the neighborhood after everyone hears my tale; this story may possibly go worldwide; children will speak of me and know my name!

I decide to get up and go outside when the phone rings and my older sister answers the phone, and states, "Mom, the neighbor wants to talk to you," as I leave for the park. I remember when the phone would ring, and many siblings would run to get to the phone first. This phone was placed on a built-in cabinet shelf and had a short cord to it. There was a limit to how long one was permitted to stay on this phone. I had no need to answer the phone at this age, but later, when I was older, I did learn to race to the phone. The phone would become a tool to head off trouble. "My parents are not home now; can I take a message?" This was a trick of mine that did work one time, and delayed reactions at other times. These telephones were common in every home back then, but some large homes would have two phones, and even some larger homes with three phones. When you had two phones or more on one phone line. you could pick up the other phone and listen in on the conversation. Sometimes. the little click sound would be clear, and the person would hear the other phone being picked up.

We only had this one phone in the living room. When we were outside in those days, years ago, there was a network message system built outside. Parents or older siblings would call out your name to come home. If someone outside heard this and saw you, they would shout out for you to go home. When the streetlights started to turn on, you'd better get going home as this was another calling system. So now, my name, is echoing through the neighborhood to come home.

I rode back home, put my bike in the yard, and walked toward the front door. I chased off a bird that was sitting on top of the chicken pen gate. I could have hit that bird with a rock; it was so close. As I went inside the house, Mom stated, "Dad wants to talk to you in the front room." I turned the corner and spotted my new BB gun box on the couch next to Dad. Now each step became that of glued shoes not wanting to free themselves from the floor, and I stopped dead in my tracks. I flashed back to that mean tattletale bird on top of the gate; how could it have told on me? Dad states, "Come here and sit down." I moved slowly toward the couch and sat down. Dad explained how proud he was of me on how much work I completed and the money I saved up to purchase this BB gun. I was in shock, not knowing what was coming next, so my guard was still up. Dad stated, "Grab your BB gun and let's go return it where you bought it."

We load up in the van and head downtown to that large store. To this day, I can remember how bad I felt for that salesman who sold me this BB gun as Dad explained the rules to him. Dad even told him that he should have sold me a .22 rifle instead, and I immediately jumped in and asked for one now. That was a mistake because I took the attention away from that salesman and placed it upon me. I did get grounded again for not asking to make such a purchase before going to get it myself. Then Dad tells me how these devil birds told him my intentions of what I planned on doing! "You only take life that you are planning to eat," Dad states, "and you do not know which birds we can hunt, and you cannot hunt birds in city limits." I do not recall what else was being said as my thoughts were on these tattletale birds. Maybe if they think that I will eat them they will stop tattling. My prison time has expired again, and I am free to play outside. I did get my money returned to me with a lesson on how to spend it wisely. I am still hoping I can afford a new bike one day soon.

Dad and Mom are heading downtown again to shop, and I can go with them. We went to that one store, but I did not want to go downstairs to look at bikes. I did not want to see that salesman again. Then we cross the street to another store that I have not been in before. This store also has bikes, but they are priced the same as the store we just left. I start to move down the aisles in a state of loss, just looking around, when a sparkle caught my eye behind the counter display in this sporting goods section.

Wow! There it was one, of the oldest tools known to man in modern-day polish metal technology design weaponry. Carefully crafted to specific angles to increase power, speed, and accuracy; a silver polished metal frame with a black plastic handgrip and a black foam pad for your forearm. Surgical tubing rubber bands were attached to a fork frame, along with a custom leather pouch. The new top-of-the-line wrist rocket slingshot, and it is calling to me. The beauty of this slingshot is memorizing as I just stare at it like it is going to be my first love.

"It is a beauty," the salesman tells me as I come out of my captured trance. "Yes, it is," I quickly reply. "How much does it cost?" I asked with much enthusiasm. To my surprise, it was priced reasonably, and I did have the money saved up.

This salesman even recommends a bag of marbles to use with this wrist rocket slingshot. I tell him I am just looking, but maybe will be back later with the money. With much excitement, I turned, and I leave to start looking for Mom and Dad in the store.

Again, I must hold the horses back. If I am too excited, my parents will know something is up, so I slow my approach down. When I find them, I asked, "When are we going home?" I just want to go home again and count my money to make sure I have enough.

The wheels start to turn, the saw starts to cut the pieces, and the hammer nails them together as an idea starts to build in my brain. I can ride my old bike downtown again and make another purchase. I think in my brain that I should ask my parents, but these tattletale birds will fill my parents mind with lies. I will ride my old bike that I made with other old bike parts from the yard.

In a large family, there were always parts from other bikes that the older siblings outgrew or broke. I was able to always repair my bike with most parts of bikes saved in the shed. I like to do jumps off ramps, ride wheelies, and just about everything done on a bike.

So, yes, I damage many of the bikes, and had a couple of car incidents that Dad had to pay for. I was riding a different color bike that I assembled with many parts of other bikes, when on this great day, I was surprised by an awesome gift from one of my older sisters. So out of her own heart, she bought me a stingray green bike with the banana seat. Did I love this bike I was so lucky to have gotten! Thank you, sister, for this great gift. It has been many years, and I cannot remember the reason, if there even was a reason, she did this for me. This bike took me everywhere, and now it will take me downtown for this prize slingshot.

The plan is simple again: I say I am going to the park, and then take off to downtown, which is less than a mile. With money in my wallet, I lock up my bike and head into the store. Again, with great confidence, the sale person tallies up the cost as I hand over cold hard cash to him. With the slingshot and marbles in a bag, I head toward the outside, where my bike is lock up. The coast is clear as I ride off like a cowboy rides away after saving the town.

As cars pass, they wave; children are cheering. It is like a parade; people are waving and cheering, and I even do a few wheelies! I ride back to the park to open my package and throw the evidence away in the city park trashcan. I am not going to show this to anyone, after learning what happened with my last purchase. I give this slingshot a delicate kiss on the polish metal frame as I begin to learn how to shoot this engineering wonder. Birds in the park are noisy, as though word is out of this wonder in my possession. It is easy to shoot; so smooth, and the power is fifty times greater than my last slingshot. I am perfectly accurate right out of the box with this slingshot and will bring an end of what has been going on for far too long. I head home to hide my treasure under my bed.

The coast is clear as I open that side door and bring in my gem that I hid outside near the trashcans, now hiding the slingshot under my bed. I leave and head to the park again; this time, even riding a wheelie farther than ever before. As friends show up, we start taking about different things when I mention what I saw at this store downtown: this fantastic engineering modern-day slingshot. I guess I was not the only one who saw this gem as we all talked about getting one.

A couple of days later, I start to show this beauty off, and even let some of my friends take shots. Some of my friends now also have this beauty. We plan on meeting at the park with our slingshots this Saturday coming up. While looking around in our storage building, I come across some lead BBs that were for reloading shotgun shells. I pour some pellets out into pill containers and hide them away.

These lead BBs may work awesome in the leather pouch on my slingshot. I make a slingshot out of heavy wire and give it to my younger brother, so he will not feel left out of the mix. I also find steel ball bearings in the storage building that I save for the upcoming war of tattletale birds.

We meet up Saturday morning at the city park and take many practice shots of cans and trees. On the top of that park is a large tree that is half hollow, and inside is a bee's nest. With bees flying around outside this hollow piece section, we start to shoot at the nest. The shotgun pellets do not work as well as I thought they would but do work ok on this kind of up-and-close shooting. We have lived in this town for a few years now, and I did learn that I am not the fastest kid in the neighborhood.

I could outrun everyone for the first ten to fifteen yards, but then everyone would pass me. I never did get to have a second gear, as some kids called it. As some friends and my brother got closer to the bee's nest to shoot at it, the bees became louder where I could now hear the buzzing.

I backed away, not sure what was going on, but stopped shooting and just watched. I shouted out to my younger brother not to get too close as he was using BBs. Then it happened, an all-out full attack of the bees, hundreds of them. I turn and run, as fast as I could, down the hill as the other kids gain on me. I could hear them shouting out that they are being stung. Now they are passing me with ease, hands waving around their own heads. We run to the bottom of the hill when the attack is called off and the bees return to their nest. As we all look at each other, I am the only one not stung; what a wonder. The slowest runner did not get stung. The others have many stings on them, as we all head to our homes. My younger brother has a few stingers in him as we explain what happened without mentioning the slingshots, as Dad does his first-aid class on bee sting removal. This would not be the only panic run us kids would have running down that hill on that same city park.

At another meeting with the slingshot kids at this city park, we were just shooting around when we happened upon a young couple making out at the park on a blanket. They rolled this large blanket over them hiding from the public view of what was going on. For the life of me, I will never know why or even how this all started as though we were the city park make-out police. Shots started to ring out as we started to shoot our slingshots at the unsuspecting couple. Shouts come out with many bad words ringing out from the man under this blanket. Just like the bee's nest, I started to move away, knowing this may not end as we think it will. Now, everyone has stopped shooting, and are coming toward me as we are now on the other side of the top when we hear unbelievably bad words again. In turning around, there is this young man standing there, and he is not happy. I still have a good head start on the other kids as we turn and run for our lives.

One by one, the kids start to pass me by, even my younger brother, as we now are in the street at the bottom of the hill. The last kid passes me up as he turns to run to his house, but the man chasing us follows this other kid, catching him on his front porch as I continue running away. We all meet up in the alleyway behind another kid's home, except the kid who got caught.

There is an unwritten word that you never run home when being chased for a reason you caused. Soon, that kid joins us in the alleyway, telling us we all must go apologize to this young couple. We all walk back to the park, but the young couple is walking away, and we shout out to them that "we are sorry," and the young man waves a finger to us. We would have other incidents with our slingshots, from breaking storefront windows and city lights getting shot out, but we never again shot at people we did not know.

My slingshot has passed almost everything that could happen with it, and I still possessed it. Now, my skill level is great. I can hit anything from most distances. It is now time to put away the tattletale birds that harassed me for far too many years, as I start to put the final pieces together on how I will end the war. The school district closed that big school behind our home and gave me more area to play and plan. I used chicken feed in the alleyway and in the closed schoolyard to lure in these hateful birds. I will feed them for a while, then one day, I will show up and shoot one.

I was riding my bike in the schoolyard, trying to learn a spin move. This is where I would pop a wheelie, then try to jump up with the bike, spin in the air, and land the bike again while still riding a wheelie. I came close a couple of times, but then I landed on the chicken feed I placed there, and it caused the back tire to slide out from under me. This crash was vicious; wreck slamming me down hard on the concrete, breaking my leg. I screamed out loud when I hit the ground, which caused that one older sister to notice I was in very much pain. She, with some of her friends, came running up to me. My older sister tried out her first-aid training, grabbing my broken leg and shaking it to make sure it was broken. With much more screaming from me, they decided to carry me home. Dad does his first-aid training so children will know how to do variety of splits on a broken leg. Mom intervened that it was time to take me to the hospital again. There could have been a grin on Dad's face. Oh, thank you, sister, and your friends, for carrying me home.

Yes, that same doctor is there again at this hospital, and asked for a few more nurses to come in and check out this homemade split on my right leg; there could have been a grin upon his face as he removed my split to place a cast on my right leg. Later, I would get this rubber piece added to the bottom of my cast so I could walk with it, and I would use it for a bumper.

Each year, some lucky pair of children would get picked to go to a warm state and spend time with an aunt and uncle on Mom's side of the family. Then, the rest of us would go get them later and bring them home. Our aunt and uncle had a swimming pool in their backyard, and this trip was always awesome for me. You could never really look outside for the views because there were no windows but could look out the front windshield. There would only be two children that would never get to spend the few weeks there at our auntie and uncle's home. This was that one older sister, then me, and, of course, I never did get to spend time with them alone. On one trip out there, we came back with skateboards with steel wheels on them. I was ok on these skateboards but loved my bike much more. I liked to sit down on my skateboard and use my broken leg with that rubber piece on it like a front bumper. Finally, freedom comes my way as the cast is removed from my right leg. I was back to riding my green bike again.

I have had some difficult times in my young life, but what happened next is still hard on me. After coming home to get some water from a long bike ride, I left my bike at the front gate and ran into the house to get my water.

After a couple of glasses of water, I go back outside to ride some more, and she is gone! My beautiful green stingray bike was gone and disappeared. My green bike was stolen away, the very one my older sister bought me. My life spirals down as I get Dad, and he calls the police. The hardest part was not so much that someone stole my bike, but I had to tell my sister, and it broke my heart. Eventually, I would assemble another bike out of parts with a girl's bike frame, using a broom handle to make it a boy's bike. Anger would build up in me, and the tattletale birds are going to pay the price, once and for all.

I continue to use chickenfeed in two areas, and now the birds feed freely. I wait many times in an ambush attack and stay with the steel ball bearings as ammo. While hiding by the old school building over a feed sight, nothing happens. I decided to go around to the other side of the building. It had rained well earlier in the day, and as I peek around a corner, there are two robins drinking water. I load up the slingshot, pull back the rubber tubing, peek around the corner, and the robins are still there. I aim and let fly a ball bearing, knowing what Dad has stated many times about eating what we take. The shot was a clean kill as I jump for joy that quickly faded away in what I had done. As I walk up to the dead robin, I realize I do not know which birds are tattletale birds; did I just kill an innocent bird? Is it worth it taking a bird's life out? All these emotions in me stir up a current like a river running wild. I thought I would feel different. As I buried this bird and put to rest that this war is over and I had won, but this victory felt empty. Again, I am in a depressed state in what I had done. Later in the year, we children would kill another bird; a pigeon, but we cook it at that park, having a meal. Later in life, we would get game with the sling-shot; cooking it and eating them, learning that we only take what we eat.

As I flip to other pages in this old photo album, there is a picture of me holding an open gift from my birthday. I could see it in my eyes that I was still sad from what I did, and carried that bird's death many years, and even felt worse when the truth started to come out that I have been a fool for far too long. I had been lied to for many years by adults! There are no tattletale birds; it is all made up. All the battles, all the sleepless nights planning, the death of Tad, death of a bird all because of lie's! It did not stop there. Then, I learned there is no Santa Claus! Lies, more lies; all the letters wasted my childhood crush! Wait, there is more. There is no Easter bunny; all have been lies! I have been played a fool by everyone; what can a child believe? My life changed very much back then; per-haps it was puberty, which I held on as long as I could to be a kid. I was crushed about Santa, trying to be good all the time, the wasted letters, the waiting to hear the bells; how did all the presents get there? The children talked about the presents all being the same color paper, all pres-ents coming the same night. Dad and all his sayings made more sense, and Mom still talk about God. I took a bird's life because of their lies, "a bird told on you!" All these years of fighting with tattletale birds that did not exist; am I that foolish? I had been tricked all my young life. What could life possibly bring next that could alter the course of my adulthood?

By Robert J.

THE CURSE CONTINUES

CHAPTER 5

With the birthright of life comes the life sentence of death, and time never stops moving. Some of us will have a long life, and some of us will not. Like the rising sun followed by the sunset, darkness is part of our life. If you can imagine in this way, life is a full circle as is the earth, as in a ring of gold, and life continues around and around. At birth, your soul, along with love, is placed on this ring of gold and grows until death; only then, your soul will leave this ring of gold, your body turning to dust, leaving only memories of what was. How you are place and removed on this ring of gold is by two attached silver arched bridges, which rises off the top of this ring of gold, coming together to join as one supporting a pure golden nest as if it is transparent glass cradling a diamond in the middle; like the atmosphere protects the earth with a transparent glass to view the sky and stars above. There are twelve pearl gates on the top edge of this gold nest; each gate is made with a single pearl; six pearl gates on the top of each silver arches. Why they remain closed or why they open for a moment of passage, no one really knows. Deep in the center of this diamond there is a memorizing bright great glow from the heavens where there is no beginning or end, everlasting life and peace.

When a man and woman embrace, in that moment, their bodies and souls can be bridged together, joining as one; this is love. Then, from this love, life can be created; love is released, allowing a soul to rise from this memorizing glow in the diamond, traveling through a chosen open pearl gate, down the silver arch, bringing into the body life, then onto the golden ring of life. As the circle of life begins, the chosen pearl gate closes; only with death will another chosen pearl gate will open on the top of this silver arch, allowing passage to this center of this diamond mesmerizing glow. Then and only then, a decision of one's life of what was, will be made. For those of us who have lost loved ones in our lifetime know that sometimes there is unbelievable communications of what was.

There is only one way to interact with this great memorizing bright glow in the center of this diamond known to man on this earth. I, myself, have and always will send my messages in hopes it safely reaches the one I am thinking of, in this mesmerizing bright glow, and will do so until the very last breath of mine leaves my very lips. I do this in prayer! For all the great highs, along with the very lows, the easy roads, and the roads less traveled, I seek answers through prayer. Many prayers will go unanswered, in our way of thinking. Many blessings, in our lives, are never understood or even noticed. Like my parents would state, always looking but seldom seeing, the beauty of life; always listening, but seldom hearing the things that matter most; always thinking but seldom knowing what really is important. This next page in this old photo album has a picture of Dad and Mom standing in the yard.

This is around the time Mom started the battle of her life, triggering a dark memory of mine. Some of the hardest times of my young life would forever scar deep into my heart; for we who have experienced this know we carry this a lifetime. We try to protect the heart, but we have no control of what will be. We just try to make it through the best we can; like when the news came about Mom having a terminal disease, then all forms of treatment failed, and Mom chose to come home to live out her last days. I was twenty years young then, so full of life, so strong, so brave, or so I thought. The last of her children that were still near surrounded Mom's bed in her last moments of life. As Mom looked at all of us, a smile appeared from her lips before she passed away; a memory instilled deep into me, never to be lost!

One pearl gate opens, allowing her soul back to the mesmerizing great glow. Oh, the pain! Oh, the hurt we felt in letting go! I would not want anyone to feel this experience, this site of leaving, and this pain in your heart of losing your mom, your everything!

Then a few months later, Dad's journey in life is called to an end; his soul allowed back into the one pearl gate, back to the mesmerizing great glow! Oh, the pain! Oh, the hurt! but this time, it is different to me; his soul was being called by another soul, his soulmate in life. It did not make the pain any easier to handle but brought peace with it. After Mom had passed away, Dad was just not himself. No matter what the family did, we could not replace the lost love of his life. There are many people in this world who have the great fortune to have found that special person, their soulmate. Then there are the people, like me, who still search for that soulmate. For us who have survived a broken heart along with the horrific pain that follows, we know it just takes time to live with the pain deep inside!

With a deep breath, watery eyes, and a heavy heart, a few more pages flip in this old photo album, and there is a photo of Dad and me. This photo is on my wedding date; Dad and I in suits. Dad must wear his tennis shoes because of his feet pain. So, most photos will not have any shoes in them. Dad would pass away before I was blessed with a beautiful healthy daughter, and neither of my parents would see this treasure of ours that we created with our love. I am a young man, twenty-three years of age, and my life is great; it could not possibly get any better!

The closing of the door in my face, and the failed marriage and all that I have been through, is a new pain that

I have never felt before, a different broken heart. With a lost love comes many emotions; anger is one of them and giving up is another. The devil is active in your thoughts; alcohol just feeds the demons, and no matter how much alcohol you consume, the country songs are wrong, your problems remain. Battles with the devil and demons are real, and it takes a clear mind to win. I can only thank Christ, God, family, and friends for helping me through this difficult time in my life. Although all prayers were not answered the way I wanted them to be, I survived yet another broken heart. Starting over again, renting my own place, I learned to live with another scar placed on my heart.

After the drunkenness and shattered dreams of what was, I remember that I was blessed with a health beautiful daughter. She was my sidekick when I was married to her mom, but after time, I would move north, and she moved with her mom south. I wish I could have done more for her, share more time together, just to be there and watch her grow! It seems it takes longer for a man to recover from a broken heart, or, at least, it was for me to recover. I moved to an exceptionally large city, north of this little town, trying to leave all heartaches behind me; then again, in a few years, I remarried.

A few more pages are flipped in this old photo album and photos of my second marriage. This marriage would last longer, but still, another failed marriage I would experience. Another broken heart to live through again, but this time, it was different. For I was blessed, again, with a beautiful healthy daughter, now almost three years young, and a handsome healthy son, just over a year and a half young. The closing of the door in my face of what was our home, but this time, I must turn and face my two small treasures, my children, which are standing next to their dad outside this closed door.

As that door closed with the deadbolt latching, I could see my breath escaping my lips, then gently blowing away from that door on this November cold morning. I take in a deep breath, trying to sum up all the courage from that sacred vault of my being, where my heart and soul is. That is the place where God has placed wonderful and unique characteristics into my being. You contain certain desirable qualities, which are gifts and traits seeded in you by our Heavenly Father. This is now the place I need to draw up courage and strength that I will need to turn to my two young treasures, my children!

I turn to them, going down to one knee so I can look them in their precious eyes. Their faces showed that of hurt, pain, and shock, as they grasp with their tiny little arm their possession close to their bodies. I reassure them that their mom just needs some time to herself, and none of this is their fault. Sometimes adults need time to work things out. "Mom loves you two treasures with all her heart." We will pray that she gets better and joins us soon," and I get up and hold their hands as we walk away from that closed door. Deep inside my being, I know the hardship I am about to face, tearing the heart apart, and yet again, outside a closed door of what could have been. This time, I am homeless again with two young children as we walk toward a payphone on this cold November day. The only possession we have we are carrying in paper bags. Too this very day, when I think of that moment of our lives, it still brings tears to my eyes, along with a heavy heart; one of the hardest things I have ever done was to look into those little eyes and try to make it easier for them to understand!

My son got a paper bag filled with his clothes and his favorite teddy bear on top, and my daughter's paper bag filled with her clothes and her favorite teddy bear, and my paper bag with some of my clothes, a bag of diapers, and a pack of baby wipes. I had twenty-eight dollars in my wallet and some change in my pocket, and we did not get the car keys. A journey always began with a step, but how can I take that first step with a foot weighing a ton, and strength from above as each step becomes lighter? I have two young treasures that need me to care for them. As we walk with heavy hearts to the nearest payphone, I do not even know who to call.

Thank God, the first friend I called is home, and comes to pick us up. We stay a couple of days there until another friend gives us a ride to my older sister, brother-in-law, and their family fifty miles or so south of this exceptionally large city we once called home. Then my older sister and brother-in-law drive us back south to that small town that I spent most of my childhood and young adulthood. There, we live with my other older sister, brother-in-law, and their family until we get our own place. Thank God for family, thank you all; with your help, we survived! Thanks to my friends who helped us; it meant a lot. This is how I became a single parent.

Being a single parent has all the rewards along with the hardships. I would not recommend it to anyone! Try to summon the entire love one can and keeping the family together; teaching the young ones of all the love it took between the two parents to create this treasure of life. Even without their mom being around, I did not want to make it seem she did not love her babies. I wanted to keep her in their lives, and she was a good mom to them, but later in her life, she just could not take care of them and herself when I was not around. I learned how to go without so my treasure could always go with.

Many times, you try to make it through financially; side jobs, two jobs, whatever it takes. You must be the good parent, mean parent, and involved parent, along with being sick; you still must care for your treasures.

The hardest part when you do not have the other parental involvement is you do not have the support on which decision is best. It is better that the children have a mom and dad in the house; this is what makes it a home. The advice is to allow the other parents to decide, for a change; to get a break from it all and just relax with no worries; to have that ability to say, "Wait till your mom gets home," or "Go ask your mom."

Another page flip, and there is this photo of a lady that helped raise their mom, a foster parent of hers. For my children, all their blood grandparents' life journeys had been called back home to that great bright glow. We were blessed early in my treasure's young lives that this one elderly woman took on the grandparent role. I thank her family for sharing this woman in our lives before her life journey came to an end.

I looked at another photo of us at a new house across town where we moved into, which, again, we were blessed that we had elderly people living there across the street. Again, out of the goodness of their hearts, they took on the role of grandparents for my young treasures. I thank you both. We would live there many years. It was hard for my children, my treasures, not having grandparents, or, worse yet, a mom not living with us. My treasures were teased about not having a mom living with us, but there was not much I could do about it; you cannot rush love. As time passes, your girlfriends will help as much as they can.

When one is single, as in my case, you are considered a package deal. There are other lives involved with you, so, sometimes, it is different. As you start to date, there will be questions that, after a while, you will need to answer. Is this person only girlfriend material, or can she become wife material, and then can she become a mother figure for my young children, as she is with her own children? Just as she should ask herself about me: is this more than a boyfriend material? Could he become a husband material, a father figure for children other than his own children? For package deals, we know it is different; however, we did see it work in fairy-tale sitcoms on television. There were some real-life package deals that work out for some lucky couples. I was just not one of them.

Sometimes there are too many activities going on to meet someone new; sometimes you just drag your feet too long; sometimes you move too fast, and then sometimes you put too much thought into it. Then there are the times you just let the moment pass for reasons unknown. For some of us, it is hard to believe in love after you lost at it; for me, to lose at it two times, made me way too cautious. I worry that if it did not work out correctly, I would break my treasures' heart again. This was a high risk I did not want to take for a long time! The phone rings, bringing me out of my hypnosis memory trance of my moment of long ago past, as I close this old photo album and rise to answer it.

The phone call is from the school, and my daughter is in trouble for doing something wrong. I wonder what a good parent would do, as I am not sure what I should do. After hanging up the phone, I seek an answer with prayer for me to do the correct thing. Currently, I have a seven-year young daughter, and a five-year young son. As I pick up my children from school, my daughter states nothing to me about what happened at school. So, in deep thought, I drive aimlessly around, in mostly silence, searching for an answer. I find myself driving back south to that little town I so fondly remember, where my life had started; back to where our home once stood so mighty, so filled with life; it is now an empty field, just like so many memories that are vanishing away of what once was. It is hard for me to look at once was; it is all gone, and leaves me with the emotions of sadness, loneliness, and emptiness.

As I drive away, a peace comes over comes me, but the answer I seek did not come into my thoughts. Instead of answers coming, my mind opens to the pain of what was, now all gone, all lost, giving birth to the hardship of my memories.

I could do what Dad would have done; there is a difference between a spanking and a whipping. No, these are different times, and I did not think I needed to be like Dad for this breakage of a home rule. A good talking just did not seem to fit. I needed to be better. I needed to be different. As we pull up to our home and I park the car, I was disappointed that my daughter had not mentioned what happened at school. We get out of the car and onto the sidewalk, and I am without an answer I seek. We are walking toward our home on the sidewalk with all this loud chatter and chirping noise coming from across the street from the row of cottonwood trees when it hits me all at once!

All along, I knew the answer. I have known it for years; it has been imbedded in me, lost for so many years. Deep inside me, to that very core of my being, where God has placed unique characteristics, with every beat of my life. As my mind opens the floodgates to allow all this information in, it is like the rain clouds that give way to the rainbow coming after a rainstorm. I have now been bestowed the honor and special privilege in communication with these Mother Nature creatures I have longed for so many years now past! I now possess the tools of all great parenting skills, and I can use it as I see fit. I stop in my tracks, look across the street, up into the role of cotton wood trees, where all this chatter is coming from. With a voice loud enough so my children could hear, along with the birds across the street, I now speak to these tattletale birds, knowing they will reply!

The chatter is so loud you could hear it a block away, as the birds are gathering for their migration to the South before winter arrives. "My daughter did what?" I ask very loudly. As all chatter came to a stop, as on cue, with my question, my children came to a stop, dead in their tracks, and looked at me. Then my children looked across the street and up into the row of cottonwood trees. After a pause of silence, the loud chatter begins, and starts to fill the afternoon air. I let it continue to go on for a second or two." My daughter did what?" I ask loudly again Now, I turn and look at my daughter, directly into her blue/ green hazel eyes as the bird chatter has ceased silence, right on cue. My daughter has the look of shock with her small mouth open, as she looks into my eyes for a second or two, then only moving her eyes to the row of cottonwood trees across the street.

The chatter again starts up as though the birds are having a conversation with me, as my daughter's eyes rolled back into my stare. My son looks at his sister for a moment, then to the row of cottonwood trees, then back to his sister. I turned my head again, back to the chatter coming from the row of cottonwood trees. "My daughter took what to school?" I ask loudly as the chatter comes to a stop again after my question. The chatter starts up again after a few seconds as I nod my head up and down, acknowledging their reply. I thank them for letting me know what my daughter did with a low voice and wish them a safe journey back to the South, letting them know, before they leave, there will be food and water placed outside for them.

I now turn toward my children. "We have to go inside and talk about this," I told my daughter as we all started to walk toward the house. Inside, after they removed their backpacks, I have my daughter sit down on the couch. My daughter became a chatter bird, trying to explain her actions on this day of her choices.

I explain to her that all the things in our home are all of ours; however, there are some things she and her brother are not allowed to have because they are for adults. "It is expected that you and your brother must ask before taking anything out of the home." The punishment is simple; my daughter will have to buy the bird food and feed the birds, along with fresh clean water, every day for two weeks.

I will not allow any retaliation against the birds, for they are our friends, and they will tell Dad again if either child does something wrong. I send my daughter to retrieve her piggybank that she had been saving money in, so she could buy the bird feed. As we empty the money onto the table, I asked her to separate all the coins into piles, along with stacking of the bills. We count the money to see how much there is, then place all the money into a clear plastic sandwich bag. We all head to the car when I noticed that both children look over to the row of cottonwood trees where the birds are chattering. My daughter had a mean look on her face toward the birds; it was extremely cute. The drive to get the bird seed was as quiet as the drive we had when I was searching for an answer on what to do, and I saw no reason to break the silence.

My mind raced back in time, so long ago past; that very first time that I learned that Dad could talk to these tattletale birds. I wonder what went through his and Mom's mind after I left the room that day. Did my grandparents use this very same method on my parents when they were young children? I wonder what they thought about it; did they do the same thing I did and try to teach these tattletale birds a lesson? That is why I told my daughter she could not retaliate against the tattletale birds. I did not want her to do some of the foolish things I did. To my parents, who told me not to retaliate against these tattletale birds, they did not know that I would. I guess they did not think I would go through so many extreme measures to be the child that would stop these creatures from telling on us young children. As we pull into the store parking lot and park the car, some birds fly up and away.

Exiting the car and walking toward the store, I had to make a comment, which so easily escapes my lips with the greatest of ease. "There sure are a lot of birds out today watching out for you all," came my statement. I got no response, but my daughter's body shrugs after the comment; there could have been a grin upon my lips. This store would not carry a lot of wild bird feed, so we just got canary bird feed. My daughter brings the bird feed to the sales counter, setting the feed there along with her bag of money. The sale clerk asks, "Do you have pet canary?" as the clerk rang up the total. "No, I do not have a pet canary; we are just feeding the birds before they fly South" my daughter replied. "That is so nice of you all to do that" came the response. We thanked the clerk and left; my daughter would have some money left over to put back into her piggy bank as she grabs the bird feed, and we head back to the car. This time, on the ride home, I break the silence.

"There are birds everywhere in this town, in this state, all around this beautiful world. These birds are gifts from God placed on this earth to help with this planet; also, to help parents watch over their little treasures. They are only doing their job, so do not be mean to the birds." I told them as we drove back to our home, surprised, with no questions.

As we pull up to park the car, the birds are still chattering across the street in that row of cottonwood trees. Should I attempt another conversation with these very same birds, or should I not tempt faith and just let it go?

As we get out of the car onto the sidewalk, the chatter is loud and clear. I now know what to do. Again, I stop and look across the street to that very row of cottonwood trees, where this chatter is coming from. With a loud voice, I answer the birds, "Yes, my daughter did buy you bird feed," again, the chatter stopped right on cue. I remain silent for a few seconds, only to continue as though they are speaking to me. "You want some bread also?" I ask them.

Again, everything worked perfectly. I am having a conversation with the birds. After listening to the bird's request, we continued into our home, where I allowed my son to go play outside in the fenced backyard. As my daughter and I get things ready to feed and water the birds, we have a conversation about how much she should give them. I believe she will be ok with the birds; she is getting used to the fact that they are what they are.

She has accepted the fact she got caught, and will do her punishment without the whining, like so many kids would have done, including her own dad. I am incredibly lucky to have children this good and understand; this is a blessing. I thank God they are not like I was when I was young. My mind wonders back in time past, when I was told these tattletale birds were just a myth.

When a child gets to that certain age, and all childhood beliefs start to come to an end, thinking about these things, like tattletale birds, can be overwhelming. Some of us kids try to hang on longer, not wanting the future of adulthood. Then we start to learn that Santa Claus is not real; there are emotions of change, a magical world of what was does not exist. We all know this emotion of disbelief; how could this be? Now, when I was around that age, I learned that tattletale birds did not exist either, just like Santa Claus was a myth, and there was no Easter bunny. I had emotions of disbelief. Had I been a fool all my life? I felt all those emotions of what are real and what is not real. My daughter asked me another question, bringing me back out of this memory to this present time as I suggest where to place the plastic bowl filled with water outside in the fenced side yard.

I never claimed that I was a smart man, nor a good parent. I just happened to have good children. However, I know that I am wrong; tattletale birds do exist, and parents can talk to them. Just like Santa Claus does exist, not in the form of body, but in the form of belief, in a form of love. Jesus defeated death, Jesus spoke of love; one cannot see love, one cannot taste love; love can only be felt in the heart, deep in one's core of their being, where God has placed wonderful things and characters traits. There, love is giving life, and with life, all things are possible. The struggles are real, and I had my share. I pulled myself up out of the mud many times, and I did slide back in, but I never gave up. Sometimes you just need to rest for a bit while in the mud hole, to gain strength to start and climb out. I know the sound of my voice made these birds stop chattering; it was a natural reaction of theirs. Tattletale birds are much more than just birds; it is a communication network between people, to the person they are trying to reach, to protect our treasures.

It is not about a nosey person or minding your own business; it is about watching over everyone's little treasures, keeping them safe and out of trouble. Children will be children, and anyone of them may do things that shock their parents, for I know this experience all too well. It is about a community, a neighborhood helping little children stay safe from their actions and actions from evil adults; a phone call will help parents. We are not born parents; we only try to be as good or better than our parents were in raising us.

I am deeply sorry for all the people that I have hurt in my life, and I truly apologize for this, asking for forgiveness. As I forgive all that have hurt me, in the name of Jesus Christ, I pray. Now, I pray that I can use this tool of the tattletale birds' network to become a better parent, a better person.

We took too many things away in this great country of ours that are good for everyone; prayer in schoolrooms removed, and the Ten Commandments out of the court rooms, to name a few; allowing the movement of the antichrist to grow and get stronger. This world is moving faster than ever before as it is going to be extremely hard on our children. There is not anything wrong with being guided by Christ and God, and sometimes we may not understand the direction we are headed toward. I know what I must do now, knowing that I placed the tattletale birds curse upon my children, just as it was placed on me so many years ago, and was probably placed upon my parents when they were young.

It is only right that this tattletale bird curse be placed on my grandbabies in the future, and if I am still on this great earth, I hope I can witness this. "No, do not place the feed so close to the water; the birds can be messy," I tell my daughter.

I move to get some slices of white bread for my daughter so she can tear them apart into smaller pieces to feed the birds. I do have some fear deep within me; can she handle this curse in a better way than I did? I send her outside to finish up with the feeding of the birds as I watch her through this large kitchen window. As she is tearing the bread into smaller pieces and throwing them down in different places on the concrete, her younger brother comes up to her and asks her what she is doing. "You know, I have to feed these birds that told on me and I hate TATTLETALE BIRDS!" my daughter replies. And in this precise moment, the curse of the tattletale birds continues to live. As I turn and walk away from that large kitchen window where I was watching and listening my two youngest children outside in the yard, there was, perhaps, a grin upon my lips!

The End.

By Robert J.
1 John 4:1-3 and Mark 10:27

EPILOGUE

MAKING A DIFFERENCE FOR OUR TREASURES

The pilgrimage of life brings growth with maturity for each of us in our own way. Children will be children, and must be watched, for they will make mistakes, and some that can be deadly. I guess I am lucky that this curse of tattletale birds was placed upon me. In so, I was able to use it on my children, making a moment in our lives better, or, perhaps, easier for me. I have made many mistakes as a child, as a young and older adult in my life, and some, which I am lucky to have made it. I was ornery as a little boy, and many tales in this short novel are true, with many tales left out.

As a young man in my teens, I broke through the ice while ice fishing, trying to jump across a large open gap in the ice, only to have reacted fast enough to get my right leg on top of the other side of the ice, which held my weight and kept my leg in place so I could pull myself out of the water up on top of the ice to safety! For many years, I did not realize how close to death I came on that day, never to understand what a blessing I got.

I try to keep my treasure safe but could not have done it without the help of family, friends, and good neighborhoods. I never understood our blessings. I just thought it was luck. I have learned that it takes a mom and dad to raise children, for we who have done it by ourselves know this. We also know if the neighborhoods stay involved with the children's safety, it will be a better place to live.

119

For evil is here, and many have no fear of God. If we stand together, we can bring back what has been lost in this fast-moving world.

For I have felt the presence of lost life beside me. I saw the presence of what was, a sunken image into the couch as though someone was sitting there, then a text; another lost family member; I believe, a visit from Mom. If we, as a community, lose faith of what is right, we lose life for our children. Let's us come together in raising these treasures of ours; keeping them safe and teaching them that it is ok to believe, for God is a creator, not a genie, and Jesus defeated death.

Darkness gives way to the light, and time never stops. I have wondered many times in my life if I got to tell Dad that I loved him. Dad was a strong man, and stood for what was right, and his actions showed us that he loved us. Mom was more the loving kind; her hugs are still missed. Sometimes, I just do not tell my children enough that I love them, and, perhaps, I am not much of a hugger type. I needed help raising my children, but we survived. I was never big on going to church as an adult, but as a parent, I did take my children.

We prayed a lot outside, among the trees, with Mother Nature. We need to bring back faith; the church needs to become an inspiration again. Parents need to teach children that there are consequences for their actions. It is all about the safety of our treasures and protecting them. Perhaps we need more tattletale birds than ever before, keeping an eye out for all children.

Mom and Dad, I love you and thank you. I hope I made you proud!

To my sisters and brothers, thank you with much love; you made it great for me. I did have it made with so much fun being part of your lives!

To the siblings that completed their life circle, with a heavy heart, we miss you. I miss you! I am sorry for not getting this out to you before your journey ended!

To my children, how lucky am I? What a great creation you all are. I love you all with heart and soul! I hope I made you smile, with laughter of joy, and I did you proud!

To my grandchildren, I love you all! Maybe one day I will tell you tales of your great grandpa, my dad, who completed his circle before your parents were born. Now this is a great story all by itself.

To my two youngest children, I wish I could have been a better dad and mom to you! I gave it my best; it was hard, but we made it this far. I am sorry your mom did not get to know the treasures we made together, but in her way, she loves you both. Your mom wrote this many years ago before you two were born. It just seems right to place it here.

YOU

I know I cannot be with you the way I want to be.

But I am always thinking of you, and hope you are thinking of me.

And so, I send this message to the one I am thinking of.

In hopes it safely reaches you, and with it, all my love.

Sharon Marie O.

To Lisa, thank you for all that you do; you are an amazing woman! You have been a great mom to Damien and the little princess, Aaliyah, our munchkin. You are great with all the grandbabies; your wisdom is needed, and I am lucky to be with you, I love you! Damien, you are awesome and a buster; we are lucky to be part of your life. I love you very much!

To the readers of this story, I thank you very much. I hope you have enjoyed, with laugh-out-loud moments, and I hope it brought back your own memories of joy! Thank you all!

134

Thanks, LeeAnn and Lucy for the photo's and help with them!

CPSIA information can be obtained
at www.ICGtesting.com
Printed in the USA
LVHW021942201021
700977LV00004B/104